Third Eye Awakening

Adventures of a Clairvoyant Traveler

Damiana Sage Miller

I'm on my grid overseeing the universe. I can throw vibrations out into different areas. I can draw the Earth in and send positive vibrations to it. Some people feel them, others are too busy with their daily lives; they don't notice them. I can bring in other planets too and do the same.

I can jet across the universe. I'm ethereal. I don't really have a body. I can create light, sound, movement, vibration, color, matter, energy. I can create my own planet if I want to, but mostly I like to send positive energy toward planets. It ripples and gathers on the planet, but some of it just keeps going out into the universe forever.

I work with everyone. I recognize the universal connection that I have, and I have everyone's energy with me. I manipulate the negative energy back into positive energy. I take it in like a tree. I take in the bad energy and emit positive energy.

I'm connected with the plants. I'm connected with the extraterrestrials, humanity, animals, down to the smallest microorganism. I'm connected to star clusters, star planets, Light beings, gas beings, vapor beings, to all types of beings in different dimensions and different worlds. Some of them developed negative ways and some of them are more enlightened. They all share my energy

T0099389

Also by Damiana Sage Miller

Ambassadors Between Worlds

Intergalactic Gateway to a New Earth

"We wish to empower humanity and aid your planet, help give you the confidence to go forth and create the civilization you wish to live in."

—Council of Intergalactic Relations

Third Eye Awakening

Adventures of a Clairvoyant Traveler

Damiana Sage Miller

New Atlantean Press
Santa Fe, New Mexico

Third Eye Awakening

Adventures of a Clairvoyant Traveler

Copyright © 2013
by Damiana Sage Miller and NZM.
All Rights Reserved.

ISBN: 978-1881217398

Library of Congress Cataloging-in-Publication Data

Miller, Damiana Sage, 1987-
  Third eye awakening : adventures of a clairvoyant traveler /
Damiana Sage Miller.
    pages cm
  ISBN 978-1-881217-39-8
  1. Miller, Damiana Sage, 1987- 2. Clairvoyants--Biography.
  3. Parapsychology--Biography. I. Title.
  BF1283.M545A3 2013
  133.8'4092--dc23
  [B]
                                    2013004752

An anthology of out-of-body experiences by a gifted, mystic seer. Journey with the author to hidden realms of the universe. Learn to awaken *your* third eye and travel to other worlds.

Cover Art: Damiana Sage Miller
Cover Design: NZM

Printed in the United States of America

Published by:
New Atlantean Press
PO Box 9638
Santa Fe, NM 87504
www.new-atlantean.com

*This publication is dedicated to
the conscious evolution of humanity.*

Contents

Introduction

Hello. My name is Damiana. About two years ago, I began to question my life. Who am I? Why am I here? What is my purpose on this planet? These are questions that have crossed my mind from a very young age, but as I was ending college, working at a boring, mundane job, and feeling stuck in a rut, these questions became even more prevalent.

Feeling lost and lonely, looking for answers, I began to meditate daily. The meditations were a great way to clear my mind and bring balance to my life, but I was still unclear about my purpose or why I was even drawn to do these meditations in the first place. Then, during a regular meditation one day, my third eye unexpectedly awakened. I didn't know what was happening or that this was even possible. A slide show of internal images flashed before me. While the visions were quite vivid, I could hardly make sense of anything because it was all coming at me so quickly. Not only could I *see* this new inner world, but I could *feel* it as well. It was overwhelming and I broke down crying.

For the entire next day, I had a terrible headache right between my eyebrows. Two days later, I was at work when I received my first telepathic message. A "special friend" from my time in Atlantis welcomed my awakening and reminded me of the work on inner planes that I have been doing for many lifetimes. (You can read the initial channelings that I received from enlightened extraterrestrials in *Ambassadors Between Worlds: Intergalactic Gateway to a New Earth*.) Ever since that first "eye-opening" experience, I have been exploring inner worlds every day, alternating between meditations, channelings, and third eye travel. This particular book is an anthology of my early third eye adventures.

The third eye is associated with the pineal gland, a small endocrine gland located in the center of the brain. The pineal gland connects the endocrine system with the nervous system.

It also produces melatonin, a hormone that affects brain waves and sleep patterns. The famous 17th-century philosopher, René Descartes, studied the pineal gland and referred to it as the "principal seat of the soul." Others consider it a bridge between the physical and spiritual worlds, a gateway that leads within to inner realms and higher consciousness.

The third eye is also linked to the sixth energy center in the body, or the brow chakra, located in the center of the forehead. In Eastern traditions, it is simply called Ajna. When the pineal gland or third eye is awakened, it is possible to have visions, clairvoyance, prophetic knowledge, profound spiritual experiences, and out-of-body adventures (astral travel). An awakened third eye also heightens empathy allowing the person to feel what others are feeling. People who have their third eyes awakened are sometimes known as seers or empaths.

Although all of my third eye experiences are unique, a few were more memorable than others. For example, my first journey to Pleiades and firsthand experience of the Pleiadians' advanced civilization was exhilarating. It also left me with a sadness at the state of our own planet and a deep longing to help create and live in a more compassionate culture. All of the Pleiadians that I met on their own home planet were happy to see me. They projected warmth and love. Many of them welcomed me with hugs. (I had some sort of an etheric body that could experience their embraces.) I saw the homes they lived in, the theaters they performed in and, during another visit, the floating cities where they keep their technology off-planet. I also meditated with three Pleiadians on Pleiades before returning home to my Earth body and everyday consciousness.

A couple of weeks later, I was just settling into my daily meditation when I felt myself being shoved. With my third eye open, I saw an agitated, young boy who was trying to get my attention. I discovered that he had recently died a violent death and was not yet ready to leave the Earth plane. He was trapped in the astral world and needed my help. Of all my third eye experiences so far, this was the most intense and emotionally wrenching.

Another memorable event occurred when I traveled to a private retreat hosted by the ascended masters, where I was guided to bathe in a rejuvenating pool of water. A copy of myself left my body and traveled to another planet. I followed my copy to see where it was going. Later, when I reflected on this experience, I realized that while my physical body was at home meditating, my etheric, third eye body was floating in a private bath. A third aspect of myself left the retreat to explore another world. A fourth aspect of myself followed it!

A few months later, the impatient and mighty Zeus beckoned me to visit with the ascended masters once again. "Up, Up, Up," he bellowed. I guess I wasn't rising up to their domain fast enough because he yanked up the ground and everything with it, including me! I spent time with Saint Germain, Mother Teresa, Buddha, and many other wonderful beings.

Some of my third eye experiences were difficult to differentiate from my own creative imagination or vivid dreamworlds. I couldn't tell if something was real or simply existed because I created it with my mind. Sometimes my guides took me to specific places to see and experience certain things. They would often manifest themselves or arrive in my presence as a bright orb of light and I knew that I was supposed to follow it. We traveled at blazing speeds through colorful wormholes to get to our destinations. Other times, I was on my own to experiment and explore. I could travel anywhere simply by thinking myself there.

Time and space don't seem to exist when I travel with my third eye. I've visited Atlantis, ancient Egypt, and even relived some of my own past lives. I've traveled to the far reaches of the universe, explored other dimensions, and experimented with remote viewing in my own neighborhood. I believe that everyone can and will eventually have their own third eye awakening. We are all destined to raise our consciousness from lower emotional expressions to higher illuminated awareness. The path forward will free us from the constraints of dense matter as we become clairvoyant travelers in a new world.

My third eye adventures shared in this book, from Aphrodite to Zeus, are in chronological order. They occurred at the rate of about one session per week during a 10-month period starting in the Spring of 2011. Some sessions lasted about 15 minutes while others were nearly an hour long. Some sessions consisted of a single journey, like my visit to Pleiades, while others contained many adventures.

All of my third eye adventures began during deep meditations, some of which were guided. I often started (and ended) my journeys in a beautiful meadow or cave. The orb of light would meet me there to begin my astral odysseys. My father meditated with me and stood watch over my body once I started traveling with my mind. He also asked questions trying to get me to describe what I was experiencing. My voice was always faint as though coming from a distance, and if I wasn't prompted to speak, I would simply enjoy my travels in solitude. Each session was recorded and later transcribed to share with you in this book.

I hope that you enjoy reading about my third eye experiences as much as I enjoyed having them. I am still learning how to use this amazing gift. You, too, can experiment with awakening your own third eye, finding consciousness in the unconscious, reality in imagination, and waking life in the dreamworld. There is an exercise in this book to help you open up your brow chakra and explore inner realms. I hope to see you there on one of my journeys!

Damiana Sage
Santa Fe, New Mexico

Aphrodite

I see a woman. She's tall with long, red hair and she has a third eye. She's naked, with white flowers around her. I think they're gardenias.

Hello, I am Aphrodite. I come bringing love, peace and understanding. Many of us are so appreciative and happy to welcome you, to have you joining us once again working toward the greater good of Earth. You — and others like you — bring such happiness to those of us who put so much effort into spreading love around the world and the universe. There is nothing stronger or more powerful than love. Even those beings who seem harsh and critical, evil or dark, with love will come around. We must truly love those beings that seem so negative; in return, your understanding and knowledge and happiness as a human being during your time on Earth will be whole. So don't focus on the negativity, war, ego, and monetary needs, because when you love and when you're whole all basic needs will be provided for.

I see a beautiful landscape with waterfalls and wild animals. There are dark clouds and thunderstorms, but they're all in the distance. Right here, the Sun is shining and light bounces off the water in such a pretty way. There are flowers everywhere.

Try not to put a wall up between yourself and others for everyone has something to give and you can learn so much from different beings. And if you go through your life full of love, even experiences that seem negative and painful, you'll grow and learn and be protected from. Blessed be the soul that opens up its heart to love and light.

I went to a different planet with huge trees. There are ferns and moss everywhere. It's right next to the ocean. There are attractive, loving beings who are very welcoming. They all have third eyes. There are little beings and big ones. I see furry animals and there are mushrooms growing all over the place. It's very other-dimensional; I feel like I'm in another realm or on another planet. There are patterns everywhere. I can't focus on things because of the patterns. I see several crescent moons in the sky. The sky is purple.

Archangel Raphael

It's an angel — Archangel Raphael. He's got shaggy blond hair and beautiful, crystal blue eyes. He's very welcoming. I feel a lot of warmth and love coming from him.

Welcome, Damiana. Your journey has just begun and there's so much you can achieve if you continue down this path. It's time in your life and time on Earth for a new expansion and a new birth. A new chapter is about to begin in humanity's existence. Many light workers, like yourself, are opening up and becoming more receptive at this time. They instinctually feel the call in their heart because we're all connected. So, as you continue opening up, as do others, you must banish any doubt that you might have and any negativity that you might feel toward other beings, for they in their own time will awaken. But with your help and others' help, you can start fertilizing the soil for the new Earth that is brought upon us.

What are you experiencing now?

I'm seeing plant life growing along cave walls at a very rapid rate. I see a little world, a planet, on the plant life that is growing on the cave wall. I see a woman made up of constellations. She has a tear drop that is full of colors. I see another lady and a prism. These scenes are flashing before me very quickly. I see tulips or poppies. I also see a wooden boat from Roman or Viking times. It's sailing on rocky water.

Is Archangel Raphael still present? Does he have anything else to say?

Yes, he's still here. He's telling me to go through the evening full of love and life and to have a wonderful night. He'll see us again soon.

Third Eye Awakening

Don't you think that it's time to start anew? We do too. Don't underestimate the other beings on your planet, for they, like you, are feeling the call. We are working with many different beings to help soften the shift to a brighter future, which will occur whether all are enlightened or not. The change is now in motion.

It's important for beings like yourself who are aware of these changes to help create awareness in your world. It's time for the Age of Enlightenment. You must help lead your world into this new and exciting period. The Sun always rises after the darkest point at night; so too will your Earth. Although your world often seems bleak, it will renew and shine once more.

Damiana should be doing exercises to enhance her clairvoyance with the third eye. Specific meditations should be set aside for just this.

Are you seeing anything with your third eye?

I see another world and the beginning of a different civilization. It's cloudy and rainy. There are pyramids. The people are farming and enjoying the rain needed for the agriculture.

Did you travel there on your own or did someone take you there?

Someone helped me see it, but it's just in my third eye.

Are there any recommended techniques for exercising and opening up the third eye?

Listening to music while doing meditations with the intent of going places with the third eye. And then playing that same music sometimes before going to sleep at night, and letting your third eye travel while asleep. You can also give me suggestions where to go, an exercise to see if I can travel there.

Let's do that now. Travel to Neptune and describe your experience.

I broke through a bunch of clouds. I went through a lot of layers. It's really foggy and cloudy.

Travel back to the Earth and see what you can experience.

It's somber. I feel the depleted ozone layer of Earth. The Earth feels heavy — drained of a lot of its resources and energy.

Can you see any cities? Can you focus on any particular town?

I'm in the Andes. It's rocky and the air is crisp. I feel extra-terrestrial energy. I don't see anyone; I just feel the energy. I like it here, it's really peaceful. It's a good place to meditate.

What kind of extraterrestrials are in the Andes?

Maybe Pleiadians. I just feel the energy. It's good energy. I feel that they might sometimes use it as a portal to come to Earth. I feel that ascended masters come here too. I'm on the very tip-top right now. I'm coming down; it's steep. At the lower part of the mountain there are crevices and small caves, but the energy down here isn't as good as at the top.

How are you traveling? Do you have some kind of an etheric body?

I don't know. I was on a spaceship earlier, but now I can just see around me.

Is there anywhere else on the Earth that you'd like to visit?

I'm in Tibet at a marketplace. People are smiling. I don't know what they're saying, but they all have such good energy. There are animals all around. I feel that the people here live the practices that we want to achieve through non-attachment.

Does anybody recognize you?

No, I'm just observing. I'm just feeling the energy. I'm back. I don't see anything anymore.

Thank the guides and return to full consciousness when you're ready.

Creative Worlds

Wormholes

There's an illuminated orb, a being of pure Light who wants me to go with it. I'm traveling through light and there are rainbows all around. I'm going really fast through the light. There are bright colors everywhere. It's a wormhole or a vortex. The colors are coming at me really fast.

Where is this being of Light taking you?

To another world. I think my guides are helping me with my third eye travels. I can stop anywhere along the way if I want to. I just have to control it with my third eye. We stop in the universe. I see galaxies. I see our Milky Way galaxy in the distance. I'm just experiencing the vastness of it all.

A Developing Civilization

There's a planet that we're traveling toward. It's very small or I'm really big; I don't know. It's about the size of a basketball. There's a little civilization on this planet. I can watch it develop, starting primitively. The beings are developing, building cities and farms. They aren't aware of other beings on the other side of the planet. They haven't discovered them yet. They're discovering religion. Time is passing so quickly for me but it's probably hundreds of years for them. They're discovering war. The two different sides have discovered each other and are fighting. They're battling over land found between them. They're the same beings but don't realize it.

Painting with my Mind

The being of Light is telling me that I can create — I can manifest anything I want — in this state of mind, during these processes. I can create and be a creator.

What are you experiencing now?

I'm back in the wormhole going somewhere else. I'm making a new planet. I'm creating it with new animals and a purple sunset. It's like painting with my mind. I'm going into the ocean, walking on the sea floor. I have a bright glow around me so I can see. There are all sorts of interesting animals. They look extraterrestrial, unique, different from Earth sea creatures.

Eye in the Sky

Oh, there's a huge eye looking down over me. There's a giant eye in the sky watching me. Maybe it's me watching myself like I was watching that planet. Maybe it's another being, I don't know. It's just one eye. I go inland. There are massive plants, trees, and vegetation. There's a liquid pool, a mineral pool, and I drink from it. I feel increased vitality and energy.

Disturbing Images

The being of Light — the brilliant orb — is back and wants me to follow it. We're traveling through the wormhole again, going really fast. We're back in the field where I started these adventures. The being of Light is telling me that my third eye is very powerful, and while I often might see things that can be disturbing, I can always create where I want to be and go to other places. The images in everyday reality can be just as disturbing, if not more so, than some of the places I'll travel, but if they do disturb me, I can always send myself to these other worlds. The being of Light is always with me.

Are you imagining these other worlds or do they actually exist?

It's a balance between the two. I create them and they become reality. I can go to real worlds and I can make worlds that will exist within my reality. They could exist within anyone's.

What are you experiencing now?

I'm just back in the field. The bright energy surrounded me, left an impression with me, and then took off.

Bidding of God

Today, I'm working with the angels and archangels. We're trying our best to influence humanity in a positive way. We're called the "bidding of God," but it's just our purpose and calling; it's not a bidding. It's what we do, and nothing would give us more joy and purpose than trying to encourage and help others. We're made up of pure love and unconditional understanding of humanity. We try our best to subtly guide Earth beings and extraterrestrials toward enlightenment.

Oracle

Something's going on with my mind; it's running backwards. I can't describe it. It's like a shift is going on in my mind.

Is anyone present?

I feel energy, but no one's coming through.

Ask if anyone wants to communicate or share something with you.

I see a past life of mine in Atlantis. I'm meditating and there are translucent rings coming from my forehead going up into space. I'm communicating with extraterrestrials.

What did you do in that lifetime?

I did something similar to this lifetime. I was a medium between worlds and I brought forth extraterrestrial information that helped assist the development of Atlantis. Many people came to me for readings, healing, and energy. I was an oracle.

Nomads

A family of "Native American extraterrestrials," nomads, surrounded me. I had a basket of cookies. I handed out cookies to everyone in the family unit until I had only one left for myself. A little girl who already had a cookie ran up and asked me for the last one. Even though I really wanted it, I gave it to her. An elder in the group then approached me and gave me another cookie. He told me to save it until later for an adventure.

Grand Potential

Garden of Eden

The ball of energy is here again. It wants me to go with it. I'm going into a wormhole. There are flashes of color everywhere. I'm going really fast. We stop. There is lush vegetation everywhere. I can feel the essence of life in the plants and air around me. It feels very pure and innocent. We're in the Garden of Eden. I am Eve. I have a choice whether to eat fruit from the tree or not. Yes, I eat it and immediately feel grounded. I'm experiencing humanity, basic human instinct.

Humanity will always eat from the Tree of Knowledge, as they should. They need to understand the consequences of their actions. Humanity has lost trust in themselves as spiritual, divine beings and they need to gently be guided and reminded of the holy souls they are, for instead of accepting responsibility and taking the knowledge as a gift, they reject it. It feels more like a curse, so they push it away instead of using the infinite power that Divine Knowledge bestows upon them.

Dream Weavers

I'm going back into the portal. We stop. I'm with the Dream Weavers. I am one of them. We influence cosmic energy by planting seeds in dreams. I helped assist in the dream that brought you and mommy together; that's part of the Dream Weaver's job. They don't control or even create the dreams, but they help influence them in certain directions. This is also why you sometimes have déjà vu, for they give you clues in your dreams about what's to come. It's hard for us to remember in waking life. Sometimes we feel it and call it déjà vu. The Dream Weavers help us with important connections and changes that we need to make in the future. That's why it's always important to remember your dreams, because they truly are guidelines and tools to help us during our time on Earth.

Prison

I'm back in the portal with the being of light. We're traveling to some sort of chamber, some type of prison. It's a past life, but I can't make it all out yet. The chamber is made from sticks and mud. I can hear the ocean nearby but I don't know where this place is. I don't know why I'm experiencing this right now; it's tribal. I think that I've been captured and I'm going to be sacrificed. My captors are keeping me here until the time is right.

Miracle by Jesus

I left again with my ball of light. I'm traveling really fast. I stop somewhere. We're listening to Jesus talk. I'm a shepherd. There are lots of people gathered all around far and wide. He's speaking to us. There's a little, old man. He's nothing but skin and bones. Jesus is healing him and you can see him transform. He's gaining weight right before my eyes.

We can do this. We all have this power. With true faith in one's Self anything is possible. It doesn't matter what your background is, or your circumstances, or your religion, or even if you believe in a divine, higher being or a divine, higher Self. With true faith in one's Self, you can create miracles.

Private Message

We're traveling again. I'm back in the field where I started today's adventures. The ball of light is immersing itself around me. It's letting me know that it's important, even during this busy month, that I continue making time for meditations, for communications, and for clairvoyant travels, for they are all eager to continue accelerating rapidly. It is of the utmost importance that we are up to snuff, so to speak, for they know that I have grand potential.

Visit to Pleiades

I'm getting into the wormhole to go to Pleiades.

Are you traveling on your own or is somebody guiding you?

Adam (from Pleiades) is taking me. We arrive. We're in a rain forest similar to those in the Pacific Northwest, with really thick vegetation, lots of trees, greenery, and ferns. There are ferns similar to ours but different. We're walking through this forest and I can see up ahead. The forest thins and there's a city. The forest ends and there are tall buildings, but they aren't like our buildings at all. They seem fictional, like how you'd imagine something from the Wizard of Oz. The buildings are very pretty and have a certain glow to them.

There are Pleiadians around me. They are all just so exquisite, with such lovely energy, very warm, loving energy. They all smile at me. They hold my hand or hug me. They're all so very welcoming. They're all so happy that I'm here. We're walking through the city. It has an ancient yet new feel to it. It's hard to describe. It feels very cultured. They have nature and greenery built right into the buildings and the city. They're together; they don't separate them. It feels nice and is very natural. I see young Pleiadians playing together. It's a game like hopscotch.

What do they look like?

They look like human children, but they have a different quality to them, a glow to them. They don't look like humans but they do at the same time. They all have these large, engaging eyes that are warm and trusting and really have your attention. They look into your eyes. They are all so friendly.

They're wearing robe-like coats. They go all the way down to their feet and they can button up in the front. A lot of them don't have them buttoned. They go down to their hands and are very pretty. They seem very comfortable. They look like they're made of a thick silk. They have this see-through, effervescent-like quality and they're all different colors. The kids have different ones. They're very cute.

What size are the children and what size are the adults?

Most of the adults are pretty tall. I'd say they are probably seven or eight feet by our measurement. The kids aren't very tall, maybe three or four feet high. They're probably about eight or nine or ten years old, by our understanding. I'm not sure. I don't see any physical transportation. It looks like Pleiadians either walk or teleport. The sky is yellow-orange, with clouds.

There are some space ships, different ones, hovering over the planet. They're very large — massive — probably miles long, triangular in shape, almost entirely made up of windows. I'm just experiencing it all, just taking it all in.

Is this the Pleiadians' only planet, or do they have other planets in the vicinity where they also reside?

They have others. I think they have three sister planets.

Do you see any suns in the sky?

I don't directly see one, but it's light out so there must be one. Maybe it's behind one of the clouds; it's kind of cloudy. There must be one or more suns.

Are they aware of your presence?

Oh yes, they know I'm here. They're so warmhearted and friendly. And the temperature is pretty nice. It's a little muggy though. There's slight humidity, but it's very comfortable. It feels just like it does after it rains.

What are the buildings like? Can you go inside one of them?

Yes. From the outside they're pointy-looking, like in our caves. What are those called?

Stalagmites and stalactites?

Yes, the ones that come up from the ground. They're like that. And everything's natural; they have trees growing out of them, plants everywhere. I'll go into one. It opens up into a theater. They perform for each other like we do. They put on shows. This is a concert hall. They play music for each other. It's beautiful. It's very elegant. It feels so rich in culture, but it's not snooty. Everything is just so comfortable, welcoming, and unpretentious. They feel very civilized.

What are you experiencing now?

I left the concert hall and I'm walking through a park. I'm just observing all the Pleiadians. There's a playground with mothers and young Pleiadians playing together. There are other Pleiadians chatting. They look like they're probably teenagers. They're laughing and talking and just being Pleiadians. There are some really tall ones. They look like scientists, perhaps. They're deep in conversation about something. I don't know, maybe they're actually astrologers. They look really wise. They're pointing to the sky and talking.

Can you talk to them or go and listen to them?

They're talking about some other planet. They're not talking about the Earth. It's another planet similar to Earth. It sounds like they're assisting this planet as well, like they assist the Earth. It's an extraterrestrial planet. They don't have humanoids on it, but it sounds like they're also depleting their atmosphere like we are and need outside help.

What are you experiencing?

I'm just taking it all in. Just give me a moment. I've come to a neighborhood. There are homes, but not like ours; they're hovering a couple feet off the planet. They're all very similar in size. They look very comfortable. I don't see million-dollar mansions or little shacks. They're different, but they're all around the same size and nicely constructed. I don't see any Pleiadians living on the street or experiencing negative effects. They all have such positive vibrations. They send out these vibrations to each other and to me. The vibrations are uplifting.

I'm watching a Pleiadian in her garden with different kinds of vegetables. They look like root vegetables, like turnips and radishes, but they're different from ours. She's picking them out of her garden. She has a basket that she's putting them in.

Did you say she was an artist?

No, I didn't. She's a gardener. There are artists, though. I saw some in the park. All of the Pleiadians that see me are so happy to see me. They're so welcoming. Many of them shake my hand and hold my hand and give me hugs.

Are they amazed that somebody from the Earth has come to visit them on their planet in Pleiades?

I think they're pleased, they're just really pleased. They are so loving. They're so nice. They have such soft features.

Do you see any animals or pets?

Yes. There are birds like our birds and small squirrel-rodent creatures that are running around. I've seen a couple of them. And one Pleiadian has an iguana (laughs), or something like an iguana, I guess. I don't know if it's an iguana. He has it on his shoulder with a little leash on it. It's really big. I haven't seen any dogs or cats, though. This doesn't mean that they don't have them. I just haven't seen any.

They do have cat-like animals. They aren't like our cats, though. They're more like a mix, maybe, between our cats and a lynx. They're bigger, about the size of a good dog, and slimmer. They have these long legs and pointy ears like lynxes do. They're the color of a tabby, but they have stripes and spots. This little Pleiadian girl has what looks like a hedgehog but without quills. It's like a fluffy hedgehog. She's playing with it. It's really cute.

Pleiades is such a natural place. It's very developed but not in a negative way. I don't see pollution or street Pleiadians. Everything is so futuristic, but it's positive, like they've developed such a natural way of living. I don't hear noises that are upsetting to the ear. I don't see anything that I don't like. It's really beautiful.

What are you experiencing now?

I'm going to sit down and meditate with some Pleiadians. You should join us. They're leading me in a meditation. [Several minutes elapse.]

What are you experiencing now?

Violet light all around me. It's emitting off of me into the sky. We transported somewhere. We're on a huge rock. I can look up and see the sky, but all around me are these huge rocks jutting up to the sky. There's water beneath me. I'm right next to an ocean. I'm in a cove and there are these rocks going up. They're probably 500 to 1000 feet high. I'm on these rocks and the ocean is behind me.

There are three of them.

There are three of what?

Pleiadians. We sat down to meditate. Then we arrived here. Adam is one of them.

Who are the others?

One is really tall. He has a dark complexion and a long, gray beard. His name is Desmond. And there's a female. She has jet-black hair. Her skin is a lighter tan. She's really tall with bright, green eyes. Her name is Lenore. I'm hugging them goodbye and I'm getting back into the portal.

What are you experiencing?

I'm just laying out in the field.

Is anyone with you?

No, it's just me.

Does Adam have anything to say to you before we end today's session?

Adam's not with me, but he loved, really loved that I came to see his planet, and he would like to talk again soon.

Conversation after Pleiades

You were very quiet. I could barely hear you.

Oh, I didn't realize that.

Because you were deep.

It seemed normal to me.

It was emotional for me. How was that for you?

Really nice, beautiful.

When did you realize that you were going to Pleiades? How did you feel when I was working with you on the guided meditation?

I was gone for that. I wasn't really listening to you.

So you had already gone deep. Where did you go?

I don't know. I was just meditating and going deeper. Then I went to the field.

So you went to the field, and then what? Did you feel Adam?

Yes. Adam met me in the field. We went into the wormhole and took it to Pleiades. We landed in a forest that was very similar to the Redwoods and the Pacific Northwest. It was very moist and thick. There were plants that looked like the Sun. They had huge leaves arranged in star patterns on top of each other. We walked through the forest and came to the city.

Was it Naor from Lazarus or the Pleiadians who said they didn't have buildings on their planet?

Naor said his planet was like a park.

Apparently the Pleiadians have buildings.

They do, but they're not like our buildings. They went up like stalagmites and were really tall, but they were all very natural. They had trees growing out of them and they were built into the landscape. It wasn't like they bulldozed the landscape to build their homes. They felt very ancient yet futuristic.

The session was pretty long. You were on Pleiades for about 40 minutes. That's not counting the guided meditation. How did you travel around?

I guess I was walking.

Walking in what, your etheric body?

I'm not sure, but a lot of the Pleiadians were shaking my hand and holding my hand, both hands, and they were just so happy to see me. A lot of them were giving me hugs. They were so grateful and pleased that I was there. I was just observing a lot of them. I was in the park watching the kids play. The houses were like domes floating above the landscape.

Was everything vivid? How clear were your visions and ability to see?

Yes, it was pretty vivid — dreamlike, but vivid.

You went into a concert hall?

Yes. It was a really huge concert hall.

Were you able to hear any of the music?

There wasn't any music that day, although I heard music outside. The concert hall was huge. It went way back, with a huge mezzanine and lots of seats for Pleiadians to come and listen. It's really beautiful. It felt so sophisticated and cultured.

Then you were out in the park. What did you see in the park?

There was a playground with moms and dads and Pleiadian children.

Did they notice you?

Some did and some were just doing their thing.

What did they do when they saw you?

They were just looking.

That's the same thing we'd do — stare — if we saw a Pleiadian walking down the street. (Laughter) What did they do when they saw you?

They gave me their full attention. They all have these huge eyes. They weren't just giving me some of their attention but all of it.

Were you self-conscious?

No, I wasn't. And there were these two older Pleiadians that looked almost wizard-like. They were scientists or astrologers, I don't know. They were discussing another planet.

Was this other planet also depleting their atmosphere like we are? Do they want to help that planet, too?

Yes, they were discussing that. Then I was with Adam and two others doing a meditation in the grassy park, so I joined them.

What was that like? How did you meditate?

It was really, really nice, peaceful.

And then you ended up somewhere else?

When we came out of meditation, we were on a huge rock. These enormous rocks were jutting up all around us.

Were they cliffs?

Yes, I guess they were. You could look straight up and see the sky, but they were all around me. And then the water was splashing up against my rock. I was higher up, too, but the water was lapping up against this cove. There was purple light emitting off of me, a violet flame.

It was radiating off of you? Were you still meditating?

Kind of.

Why did you meditate with these other Pleiadians? Who were they?

I don't know. They were just kind, friendly Pleiadians.

Were they Adam's friends?

Yes. I feel that they're ambassadors, other ambassadors who are very spiritual, highly enlightened.

It's such an honor to meditate with Pleiadians on their home planet.

Yes.

You saw some animals. One was on a child's shoulder?

Oh, the iguana.

But he had it on a leash?

He had it on a harness but it wasn't going anywhere. It was just chilling on his shoulder. (Laughter) But the little girl had a small fluffy hedgehog type of animal, a little fluff ball. She held it out to me.

Did you take it?

No, I just watched. She was showing it to me.

Wow. And Pleiadians have big eyes?

Yes, and very soft features.

Perhaps that's because they're not always quick to argue and ready for battle, like we are on Earth.

Yes, their features are not hardened. And their eyes are huge and deep.

Do they take up more of their face?

No, not really. They're just deep and entrancing.

Do Pleiadians have ears?

Yes. They're very humanoid looking, but they look different from us.

Are they thin?

They're thin. I didn't see any overweight Pleiadians. (Laughs)

I bet they don't eat processed food.

(More laughter) They're thin and very tall. The kids were similar to my height. But most Pleiadians are pretty tall, around seven or eight feet, I'd say. They look human, yet there's something different about them. I don't really know what it is. The energy they emit is different.

Are their eyes turned up in any way?

They're just big. Have you ever seen someone where you just can't stop looking at their eyes?

Are they shaped like ours?

They're shaped like ours, big almond. But it's like when you look at someone and you can't stop staring at their eyes. There's just something about them.

Do they have noses like us?

They have noses and mouths.

Well, Adam said that our gene pools are similar.

Yes, very similar, but there's something different. I think they are more developed. They're all very attractive. I didn't see any ugly Pleiadians.

Did you see any homeless Pleiadians?

I didn't see any homeless Pleiadians.

Are you sure that they didn't just take you to the best neighborhood? (Laughter)

I'm sure.

You said there were three Pleiadian sister planets. Is that the sense that you had?

Yes.

When they say that they're Pleiadians, that's just a way for us to identify with them. But when we look up at the Pleiades or any other cluster of stars, it's just one section of the sky. It continues on into deep space beyond where we can see. A Pleiadian planet could even be in another dimension in that general region from our point of reference.

Yes.

We can say the same about Naor from LaZarus, whose home base is north of Orion. That's for our reference. We can see the stars of Orion, but not the stars beyond the Orion constellation or in another dimension.

What made you so emotional?

The idea that you were having a firsthand experience with advanced beings from another civilization. This is extremely rare, a very unusual experience. Your descriptions are vivid. I don't know how much of it is your imagination and how much is real, but I believe it. When Adam communicates with us (as in *Ambassadors Between Worlds*), he uses a different vocabulary. He puts ideas together in ways that I've never heard you speak before. Now, you've described firsthand experiences with the Pleiadians. They're all very happy to see you, to have you visiting. It's very emotional.

Yes.

Maybe they're my brothers and sisters. You know that I've never felt very connected with Earth. I've had some lives here, but I feel like I'm from elsewhere. Maybe you're touching into some of my closer family and that's what's making me emotional.

Yes, I feel that way, too. Thank you.

That was a great experience, another positive session. Thank you.

Follow-up with Adam from Pleiades

Good afternoon, my space siblings. How are you this fine evening?

We're doing well, thank you.

I did enjoy taking Damiana back to my home planet and showing her some of our life and activities (aside from talking to humanity through open vessels like Damiana, of course). I take it you'd like to do a follow-up session and have some questions about the journey.

Yes, thank you. It was a wonderful experience that was soul-stirring and emotional. We couldn't stop thinking about it all week. My first question is about the traveling process itself. Damiana and I would like to know what actually occurs when she travels with her third eye. What is traveling? Is it her mind or does she have some sort of an etheric body?

It is somewhat of a mixture of the two at this time, but it will change as she develops the process. It will go more toward, yes, an etheric body. Right now it is a mixture of her mind's eye and an etheric body that she creates with her mind's eye. She is at this time experiencing certain places and viewing the contents. As she continues developing this process, it will become easier and clearer and more ideal.

When you say that "she is at this time experiencing certain places," do you mean as we speak now? Is Damiana actually traveling with her third eye and having other experiences while you and I are talking?

Damiana is present at this time. However, she will in the future be traveling to other places while we have our discussions, when the timing is right.

When Damiana went to Pleiades, she experienced handshakes and hugs from many wonderful Pleiadians. How was that possible?

> *It's this process of the etheric body where she is not only seeing, but also experiencing through feeling. She is extremely connected to senses, and not just her visual third eye. And so through these experiences she can create and feel the atmosphere of these exchanges, including meetings between other beings and sensory feeling of her surroundings.*

Was Damiana's description of Pleiades an accurate description of your planet?

> *Oh yes, Damiana was present on our planet. However, it was not completely whole, for it's like you watching a film on Thailand and describing it as you're watching it. You're going to leave out some parts. However, she was accurately describing what she saw.*

Damiana described the buildings as natural, and similar to stalagmites with points at the top. Can you explain what these buildings are really like and perhaps what they are made of?

> *On our planet we find it very important not to alter our environment — to maintain our roots — while still creating and developing a more technologically-based civilization. So we try our very best not to interrupt the natural flow of our planet. Many of our buildings are built like your termite mounds, and these are what Damiana was viewing. Termite mounds have a very secure bottom structure and then rise to the sky. They were created through layering and by using the environment as best as we can. We built these buildings out of natural, planet-based material similar to your clay or adobe, as used by many Earth-beings in the past.*

Damiana said the homes seemed to be levitating above the ground. Can you explain this?

*We have tapped into the magnetic fields within our
planet. This has enabled us to not deplete our environment by creating homes right on top of it. We are able
to have the environment continue growing around
us and underneath our homes without destroying it.*

On Pleiades, Damiana saw gigantic space ships in the sky. Can you
explain what these were doing up in the sky?

*We are very technologically advanced, however
we choose not to have our most technological advances
placed upon our planet to destroy our environment.
So, much of our civilization lives off our planet, not
directly on it. Many Pleiadians live in these spaceships
and come down to the planets to interact and socialize.
These spaceships are stationary around our planet
and have whole cities and towns within them.*

My next question is similar to an earlier one. Damiana seemed to
experience the weather on Pleiades. She described it as humid. How
is it possible for her to not only see with her third eye, but to experience
the weather as well?

*Again, she is in between these viewing and ex-
periencing stages of her third eye travels. She is
immersing herself in the senses and experiencing,
through viewing, all the senses. So, through this she
is able to observe and translate the observation into
touch, smell, taste, and hearing.*

Damiana listened to two wise beings on Pleiades talking about another
planet. Who were these beings and what were they discussing?

*We have many philosophers and scientists on our
planet who assist many different planets, as we do
with your planet. The two philosophers that Damiana
was observing were discussing a planet similar to
yours. Although it does not have humans on it, small
extraterrestrials called Lenoidals live there. They are
very similar to the Grays in personality and technology. They are similar to the humans in their*

advances through dimensions, for they, too, are depleting their atmosphere and need assistance. We are ever eager to help.

What do you mean by saying that they're similar to humanity in their advances through dimensions?

They are also in the third dimension. They are thousands of light years away from you, but they are experiencing shifts similar to what you are experiencing on your planet.

Damiana saw animals on Pleiades. What other types of animals do you have?

We have many animals like you do on Earth. We absolutely enjoy and love the pure spirit and compassion that animals share. We have many animals that you have on your planet, as well as extinct ones that you once had. We also have animals that have mutated, or adapted from their environment, into different creatures.

Damiana meditated on Pleiades with you and two other Pleiadians who gave their names as Desmond and Lenore. Who are these beings?

Desmond is a dear friend of mine and Lenore is my younger sister. We all enjoy accommodating human beings and were very excited to share a meditation in our world with Damiana. Her presence on our planet was both very enlightening and encouraging. Desmond, Lenore and I, as well as many other Pleiadians, enjoy daily meditations as often as possible.

Do you have any tips for Damiana to help her develop and control the use of her third eye?

Continuing on these journeys will help bring back an already developed muscle. She has experienced quite an awakening already. Focusing on and describ-

ing these experiences will continue the development
of her third eye. Also, make sure to alternate between
the travels, the channelings and the meditations, as
I know you do.

Do you think it would be wise for us to include some personal readings for people in the mix?

I think that would give Damiana lots of encourage-
ment, as well as help humanity. So, yes, I do think
that experiencing and experimenting with all aspects
of this gift would be quite vital to help move along
this channel.

I have several questions on other topics. [These are discussed in Damiana's first book, *Ambassadors Between Worlds: Intergalactic Gateway to a New Earth*.] Before I ask these other questions, do you have anything else you'd like to share with us about Damiana's experience on Pleiades?

It was quite a gift to have her. We would enjoy
sharing more parts of our world with her in the future.

Absolutely. I know that Damiana would love to return to Pleiades, so we'll definitely plan that again soon.

Third Eye Exercise

Good afternoon. It is I, Naor. How are you on this fine day?

Hi Naor, welcome. We are doing well, thank you.

Today, I would like to take you on a guided meditation to help Damiana with her third eye travels, and perhaps encourage others as well. Is that all right?

That sounds excellent. We look forward to today's session.

Start off by focusing on your breath. While you're focusing on your breathing, turn your visual eyes upward toward your etheric third eye. (Your eyes should be closed during this exercise.) Continue with the breathing. Breathe in through your nose, then visualize yourself exhaling out of your third eye. Do this for about four minutes. Next, breathe in through your third eye, exhale through your mouth.

Now, let's begin. Inhale through your nose, exhale through your third eye. After a few minutes, inhale through your third eye, exhale through your mouth. Continue focusing and giving purpose to the third eye position on your forehead. For the last few minutes, inhale and exhale through your third eye.

Doing these third eye, breathing meditations for just a short amount of time every day will help encourage and control the flexibility of your third eye.

Stuck in the Astral World

[I started today's meditation like many of my others. A few moments later, I was startled by the presence of a little boy trying to get my attention.]

There's a little kid who's trying to push me.

[Several moments pass in silence.]

What are you experiencing now?

I'm trying to hug this little kid. He's really upset.

What is he upset about?

I don't know.

Ask him.

[Damiana cries uncontrollably.]

What are you upset about?

He's a burn victim. He burned in a house. He's just six or seven years old.

Why are you having this experience right now?

I don't know. I think he needs my help.

How can you help?

[Long silence.]

What are you experiencing now?

I'm just trying to love this kid. He's upset and lost.

Is he alive? When did this burn take place?

I don't think he's still alive.

Did he recently pass away? Is he confused about having passed from life to the other side?

I think so. I don't know what happened. I don't think he does either; he's confused and angry.

See if you can access his akashic records. Call upon your guides to work with you to see what you can do to help this boy.

[Long silence.]

What are you experiencing?

He has an older sister. She was in the house with him. He's stuck in the astral plane right now. I don't know if she is stuck as well or if she has moved on.

See if you can take them to their guides.

We're going back to the house looking for his sister. It's all burnt.

The house is burnt?

Yes, it's completely destroyed.

Where is the house located?

It's in a rural setting. I don't know where it is.

Where are the parents?

I don't know. I get the sense that they weren't in the house, just the little boy and his sister.

Are you back at the house?

I'm in the house.

Do you see his sister there?

I don't see her.

Maybe she moved on and is with her guides.

Maybe.

Where are the boy's guides?

We're going to find them. He wanted to go back to the house first. He doesn't want to move on until he finds out about his sister.

Take him to his sister. Call upon your guides to work with you so he knows that his sister is okay.

His sister is safe. She's moved on, but he doesn't believe me.

Are you able to connect him with his sister? Is there a way to show him that she's okay?

[Long silence.]

What are you experiencing?

Jesus.

Is Jesus with you?

I'm trying to get the boy to go with Jesus. [Damiana cries.]

It's okay, Damiana. Did the boy go with Jesus?

[Long silence.]

What's happening now?

I'm trying to get him to go with Jesus.

Why did the boy come to you? Why are you two together right now?

He needs my guidance. He's confused. He doesn't understand what happened.

Does he trust Jesus or is he having a hard time with this?

He's having a hard time.

Does he trust you?

Not really, but more than Jesus.

Can you _will_ yourself to his sister?

I'm having trouble locating his sister. I know she's on the other side.

Ask Jesus to help you.

[Long silence.] I'm bringing his sister to him.

Is he with his sister now? Is he a little bit more calmed down?

Yes.

Is he a little bit more at peace?

He's going with Jesus. They're all going, the three of them.

Is Jesus taking both of them?

Yes.

What are you doing now? Are you with them?

No, I'm back in the field.

Are you ready to emerge or do you want to stay in the field a little longer?

I want to come back.

Bring yourself back when you're ready.

Conversation after
Stuck in the Astral World

Well, that was an intense experience. We don't yet fully understand the different aspects of your gift or where it is leading. However, your very first channeling said that if you continued down this path you would see things that cannot be unseen that might be difficult for you since you're so emotional.

When I was going deeper into my meditation, I felt the boy pushing me off the couch. I could physically feel it.

Why did he push you?

He was upset, angry, and confused.

How old was he?

About six or seven years old.

Was he directing his anger at you or just trying to get your attention?

I'm not sure.

Did he eventually trust you?

A little bit when Jesus came, but he was extremely upset, very angry.

He wanted to see his sister? Were they together in the house when it burned down?

I could smell it.

You could smell the fire?

Yes. It was an extremely disturbing smell. Everything was burnt. I could smell the ashes, the burnt house, the burnt wood, and probably even burnt flesh.

I understand that this was somewhat of a traumatic experience for you. Perhaps we have to learn how to adjust and separate your emotions. Doctors at a trauma center and detectives at a homicide scene must learn how to emotionally protect themselves to remain professional at their work. I don't think the answer is to block out these experiences from occurring but rather to learn the fine points of your craft, how to separate yourself from emotional involvement, truly embracing the idea of non-attachment. You can be sensitive, helpful, and compassionate regardless of how you're called to serve, yet remain non-attached from others' personal experiences and karma. It's not necessary for _their_ experiences to be _your_ experiences except for the helping and serving part.

This was such an unexpected event. I'm sure the guides know what they're doing by making this experience available to you. This is the beginning phase of us dealing with this level of emotion. We must learn to step back from whatever it is that you're going to see with your third eye or whatever you're eventually going to be doing with your third eye travels. You know, this is sort of like midwifery work on the opposite end of the spectrum. You just helped a confused soul that passed away to make the transition in a more comfortable, peaceful way. Instead of being a midwife to souls coming in, you were a midwife to this soul leaving. It's interesting that you recently talked about becoming a midwife.

Yes.

We'll have to explore this experience a bit more, perhaps get a follow-up session with one of your guides. It was pretty intense. I'm still trembling. Your third eye is not usual. Whatever is going on with your third eye is not a common development on this planet, at least not in humans. Do you have any sense about when the boy's death occurred?

It seemed recent, but I'm not sure. It felt like it happened in rural farmlands. The parents weren't in the house.

Were the kids just there by themselves?

I sense that the kids set the fire.

Wow, there is so much pain and suffering on this planet. I suggest that we take a five minute break and then reconvene for a meditation.

That sounds good.

Follow-up with Adam
(Stuck in the Astral World)

Good afternoon. We are always humbled and honored by these encounters, for your planet is headed in an undetermined direction and it is up to light workers, such as yourselves, to create the change and provide the footsteps toward a brighter future for humanity. Don't underestimate these exchanges and the calling each and every one of you has, for you truly are being asked to set the stage for change for all of humanity, being ambassadors in this time of change.

We are continuing the process of working with Damiana, always pushing the envelope to exercise a long-forgotten gift. So, different exchanges, like today's earlier session, push her in many different directions until we settle on one that is both uplifting and most appropriate for her and her service toward humanity. Don't underestimate or overlook your gifts as well, for they, too, will be at the forefront of change throughout humanity. And the work you've already done — and the work you will return to — is of the utmost importance for providing guidelines and painting a picture for an ideal civilization. Digesting these interactions can often be overwhelming, but I am proud of how well each of you are handling them with such dignity and respect, constantly making time for these important works to be transcribed and relayed. We thank you for that.

Damiana, what are you experiencing?

I'm just trying to make the connection better.

> *As the seasons change, so too shall these inter-*
> *actions, constantly getting stronger. And like the ebb*
> *and flow of nature, what is natural for your family will*
> *continue developing into a fully functional gift to share*
> *with the many people who will seek it out.*

To whom are we talking?

> *It is I, Adam.*

Can you give us some insight into Damiana's experience earlier today?

> *Damiana is just at the very beginning of experienc-*
> *ing everything her gift has to offer. It is important that*
> *she tries out different aspects of her gift until she*
> *settles into the one she's most passionate about and*
> *has most developed. Earlier today she experienced*
> *third eye travel on the astral plane and helped a lost*
> *soul find the other side. A young boy was lost,*
> *confused, and angry, for the astral plane can seem*
> *quite scary to souls who don't have it under control*
> *— similar to Damiana's first experience in this lifetime*
> *with the third eye. Her guidance helped set free a*
> *passing soul and we do appreciate her help in the*
> *exchange. Some souls often get stuck and trapped*
> *in a middle place, for they are not yet ready to let go*
> *of the Earth life. And while they are aware that some-*
> *thing has changed, they're not necessarily aware of*
> *their death, for you go to the astral plane every night*
> *in your dreams.*

When did this boy die? It seems like it might have been something that took place days or weeks ago and yet Damiana had this experience in the present, or at least it seemed to have taken place in the present.

> *Time is not a factor on the astral plane and, yes,*
> *this boy died several months ago and he has been stuck*
> *in your perception of time since then. However, time*
> *is not a factor on the astral plane, so all interactions*
> *that occur there are happening in the Ever Present*
> *Now.*

Did Damiana's spiritual guides help her to have this experience or was this a spontaneous experience? Are the guides helping Damiana's third eye to open or is this something that she is doing on her own?

> *Yes and no. The guides are always with Damiana, assisting her. She is also on her own, reworking a long, lost muscle. Today's interaction, while spontaneous, was part of our teachings, for she has many gifts. The guides are aware of all of them and find it beneficial for her to experience interactions like today's.*

Is there anything that Damiana can do to support the process of developing emotional equanimity or non-attachment to these experiences? While she desires to serve and to help and to explore these gifts, it's a very emotional experience for her. Is there any way that we can work with that?

> *That is something that will have to come with time. But it is very important that she develops an equanimity needed with these experiences, for she will see many things, if she continues down this path, that will not be pleasant but that are all aspects of humanity. So, she must gain control of her emotions and set them aside to do her work, which she will with time.*

I don't have any more questions. We were mostly concerned about understanding today's experience. It was obviously, as you can imagine, a very powerful, emotional experience for us. Thank you for coming through and sharing a few words with us today.

> *Indeed. I will be back. We will continue the teachings, the Q & A, and working with Damiana's third eye and channeling as she continues developing her many gifts. Once again, as always, I am honored to have these exchanges. I bid you good day.*

Fairies and Sprites

I'm with the ball of light. We zoomed out into the atmosphere. I'm looking down on the planet now and as I get closer my knees are brushing against treetops as I enter a forest. I'm going into a tree with little house elves and devas; it's so magical. There are mushrooms and moss everywhere. The forest floor feels like carpet because it's so soft from the moss.

Is this on the Earth?

Yes. There are sprites, fairies, and little creatures around. It's a magical forest. They have their own little world separate from ours. They view the Earth differently. It's the same planet, but a different civilization. They have their own history. They're aware of humanity's existence, but they don't interfere or let it affect their development and their own lives. They interact with the animals. They're able to speak with them. I see a badger, a wolverine, a ferret, and a skunk. Fairies ride on them and keep them like pets. The animals are huge compared to them, but the fairies ride on them like we ride on our camels.

> *There was a time when humans interacted with the fairies. Now it's just folklore and fairy tales. People don't believe in them but they're still around — in your forests, deserts, and jungles. They're abundant in rural areas. If you sit quietly, you can see them, perhaps, or feel them and exchange energy with them.*

I think that's the best part of this experience, the exchange of energy. There are beautiful flowers, absolutely gorgeous.

Floating Cities

I'm with the ball of light. We're zooming out and boarding a spaceship. I think I'm on one of the Pleiadians' floating cities. It's very different from their planet. It's where they keep their technology. They're highly advanced in technology but they don't destroy their planet with it. They have all sorts of stuff; I don't know what it is. There are lovely Pleiadians all about. This is a truly advanced city but it's in the sky, floating in a spacecraft. There are homes and buildings up here too. There are mini-crafts off some of them, like we have boats or cars at our homes. I hear interesting music. I'm going to follow it. It's incredible how much stuff they have up here. They have meditation groups — beautiful areas with crystals and flowing waterfalls. They sit and do their meditations. It's very pretty. I'm leaving now.

Crying Baby

I'm in a cornfield. There are corn and wheat fields everywhere, as far as the eye can see. I see a farmhouse, a barn, animals, and a couple of fruit trees. I see a baby and some other children. The baby is screaming. It's really crying. The farmer is about to kill, or he already killed, one of the pigs. The baby is really upset by it. The older kids are trying to comfort her, taking her down a path. There's a garden with little bunnies in it. The kids are helping in the garden, picking some vegetables. I think they're having some sort of big dinner, taking the vegetables back into the house.

Why are you seeing this scene?

I think it might be one of my past lives. I don't know who I am yet, who I was.

Star Dolphins

I'm on a rocky beach. There are seashells and driftwood. I'm going under the water to see what I can find. It's very dark. I illuminate myself. It's still pretty dark. It is cold water but I don't feel it. I don't see any creatures yet. I keep looking, going deeper. It's getting darker. I look up and can see the surface with just a glimmer of the Sun on it. I turn around. There are little fish, bottom feeders, on the bottom of the ocean. It's chilly water. I feel like I'm in water under one of the Earth's poles.

Why are you there? What's there for you to learn or grow from?

I willed myself here. I'm just experimenting with my third eye. I'm seeing where I can go.

Is anybody with you or are you doing this on your own?

I'm by myself right now. The ball of light was with me earlier. I'm just seeing where I can go with my third eye. I'm trying different things to exercise and manipulate it. It's expanding now. I can see it stretching in front of me.

There's a whirlpool swirling up and I emerge on the surface. I see dolphins, but not like ones that we know. They are star dolphins, dark blue, almost black, and they have stars on them.

Dinosaurs

I'm going back in time to when the dinosaurs existed. I see a big lake and huge dinosaurs, brontosauruses and bigger. They are hanging out in a herd. There are pterodactyls flying around, landing on cliffs in the distance. I'm walking over to the brontosauruses. I don't even reach up to their knees. I'm way below their knees. They're so tall. There are giant bugs, like dragonflies, about the size of my head. They're flying around. It's really humid. I can see flaps coming up from the water every now and then. There's a water creature. The trees and vegetation are really tall, even taller than the brontosauruses. They're reaching up and eating like the giraffes of today. There's a little dinosaur, a skinny dinosaur on two legs. It runs really fast, darting around.

Tokyo, Japan

I'm now going to zoom out, move forward and then back. I'm in Tokyo, today, and I'm watching the hustle and bustle of people all around; it's extremely crowded. It's like our New York city. It's really crowded. People are running around everywhere, in business suits and casual wear. There are lights like Las Vegas, but with really high skyscrapers. I see a bench. I'm going to sit down and watch people. Everyone's running around and talking on their cell phones. Even the little kids have them. The people are mostly Japanese but there are some Americans and people from other countries too.

DNA Grid of the Universe

Now I'm going into the universe. There's a grid, but it's twisted like our DNA. The universe is twisting it like that. I'm just going to lie on it. There are infinite strands that I can see right now, but normally you can't see them. It's peaceful. I'll come here again one day.

What are you experiencing now?

I'm just lying out in the universe. It's an interesting feeling, very comforting. I feel like I've been here, that I've done this many times before. I'm just experiencing the light and the universe. The light is surrounding me. I'm feeling the love and the light and the universe. It's a really beautiful feeling.

Santa Fe, New Mexico

I'm going to try traveling to the Santa Fe Plaza in real time, right now. I'm on the Plaza.

Are you actually on the Plaza or above the Plaza?

I'm on the Plaza. There are about 20 to 30 people here, not too many. There are still a few tourists left over. I see the fajita cart with smoke rising up. Something that is being cooked is burning. There are some locals on the southwest corner of the monument. Three of them are talking. One of them has a boxer/

pit bull mix with him. Now I'm looking over toward the southwest side of the Plaza; there are some people walking. At the Five and Dime, there's a family with four young kids. There's a cop in front of the old Ore House. There are two Native American girls eating ice cream. It's hard to say, but I feel like I'm traveling in real time.

Where are you now?

I'm on the northeast corner at the Frank Howell gallery. There's a woman bringing in some posters that they had outside. She's bringing them in for the evening.

What are you experiencing now?

I'm back in the field. I'm going to lie here for a minute and then I'll come back.

Private Message

I came back. I'm back in my body. I let the light fill me up and then I drifted back.

Where are you now?

I'm back here with you.

Are you experiencing anything? Are you getting any messages from your guides?

Yes, to continue doing these practices. To keep stretching my third eye, for we have just tapped into a very small percentage of the potential capacity of my third eye. It's quite enormous. It's important to continue stretching and willing and manifesting it, if I so choose.

Are you ready to return? What are you experiencing?

I'm just letting the energy fill me up. I'll return in a minute.

Arctic Aliens

I'm starting out today in an arctic tundra. This wind is blowing really hard and it's very cold. It seems uninhabitable, but there are beings here, perhaps an ancient civilization. I don't think they're fully human. They're probably between four feet tall and five-and-a-half feet tall. They have protective heavy coats on, and they're inland. If you go outward, you come to the ocean. I go back inland to that civilization, which is either ancient or futuristic. They have huts as well as construction built right into a cliff wall — cliff dwellings. I don't know why they chose to station here; it's so cold and windy.

Is this on the Earth in a different time period?

I believe so. It's either thousands of years ago or thousands of years in the future.

Did you come here on your own or with one of your guides?

I started out here. I don't know why. I'm just observing this civilization; they're extraterrestrial.

What are you experiencing now?

I'm on a ship that they've made. They're quite advanced in what they've created, especially if it's from a long time ago. Even if it's in the future, I feel like the Earth has rejuvenated itself in a different way. They have big boats like I imagine the Viking boats, big wooden boats with sails.

What are the boats made of? Where did they get the material?

The boats are made of wood. I don't know where they got the material. There was some vegetation growing through the snow back at the site, but maybe further inland there are trees.

What is important for you to learn from this experience?

Just the involvement of the extraterrestrials on the Earth. I'm just observing and using my third eye.

How are the extraterrestrials involved? Are the beings extraterrestrial or are the extraterrestrials working with the beings?

The beings are extraterrestrial. At least they don't look like modern-day humans. I sense that they're extraterrestrials.

Ancient Egypt

I change directions. I'm in ancient Egypt now, probably the last civilization in Egypt before the newer ones. They are using the people as slaves but there is an energy force that they use. I can see it being transmuted, transferred. I don't think that you can normally see it.

Where is the energy being transferred?

From the group of people to the Earth to the tools and the building supplies for the pyramid. I can see the energy being transferred between them. I can also see it coming from the Earth. It's a joint energy from the people. It's not an individual process at all. It's a united energy.

What else are you observing or experiencing?

I'm pondering the idea of energy and how we can use it today. There's obviously a physical energy within us that we all have. When we run or jump or move, it's energy that's being exerted. We can use that energy for positive change and an alternative source for our planet. When you run or jump or do something like that you get winded, and you might say that you're out of energy, exhausted from that, from the movement. But where is that energy coming from? We seem to have an infinite source even if we get winded. There's some sort of key within it.

Do you have any idea what that key is, how to tap that energy, how to locate or harness that energy?

I don't know, but it's there. We use it every day. We aren't even aware of it but we use it constantly. We're using that energy with everything that we do.

Perhaps we have to channel the energy, focus our mind on concentrating and directing the energy.

Yes, perhaps. We can experiment with that.

Land of Giants

I'm going into a wormhole in the universe to travel somewhere else. The colors are everywhere. I landed on another planet. It's filled with vegetation and ancient ruins. There are huge giants on this planet. I'm just a little person. The giants seem undeveloped, pretty simple right now. Perhaps they're in the beginning stages of their development on this planet.

What dimension is this planet?

I suppose it's a higher dimension. I don't think it's anywhere in our dimension, although the physicality of it isn't different.

I wonder whether higher dimensions can have more simplistic and basic civilizations.

I'm not quite sure. Perhaps simplicity can go in and out of dimensions. Or perhaps these giants, while simple-minded in intelligence, are more advanced in other aspects, but I'm not sure about that either.

Where is this planet? Do you have any idea where you are, the direction or region of the universe?

I am south if you go straight down through the Earth, if that makes sense. There are big reptiles here, too. I don't think there are dinosaurs, but there are some giant reptiles, like Komodo dragons, but larger. And they're pretty creepy, but I think they're vegetarian. The air is really thick and the sky is a grayish-yellow.

Is anyone on the planet aware of your presence?

I don't want them to be. I'm keeping myself unknown. I'm very small compared to all these creatures that I've seen so far.

Do you think they have a violent nature?

I think they have a simplistic nature. I think they just have basic instincts. I might be viewed as a danger to them, I don't know, or annoying like a bug, perhaps.

Northern California Coast

I came back to Earth, floated down. I'm on the edge of a cliff overlooking water. There's a nice breeze. This experience is a reminder of why so many souls reincarnate upon the Earth. It's really pleasant and very beautiful — just the warm Sun and a slight breeze on the edge of this cliff over the water. I'm just experiencing it, breathing in the air.

Where on the Earth is this place? What time period?

It's present time somewhere on the coast, perhaps Northern California. I'm just going to lie down and then come back.

Beginning of Time

I'm back in the wormhole. Now I'm somewhere that is totally white and empty. There's nothing here right now. It's completely empty in its whiteness.

Is it white or light?

I think it's white. I guess it could be white light, but it's white. I moved my arm and created a line within it, like on a canvas. I moved my other arm and made another slash across it. I can think and create stuff. I can make it here. It's like the beginning of time when we were just Light and manifested a world for ourselves to create physical reality. It's like a blank slate. You can create whatever reality you want. It's two-dimensional right now, but I can think and make it three-dimensional.

Can you create something?

I am creating a world and throwing Light into it. I made a sunset with moons and stars in the sky. There are animals and ocean waves. And now I've thrown "little" Lights into it. No physical bodies, just Light — pure Light energy, with depth and concepts and knowledge and ideas. I'm giving Light the same privilege that I have and they can create what they want. The Lights are now creating their own worlds and they're all different. Some of them conflict with each other. They don't match up, so they clash, but I erased them. Let those Lights start over. I guess there has to be some guidelines, even though there shouldn't be.

Well, it seems to me that the constants in the universe act as guidelines.

Yes. I'm going to leave the Lights to create their worlds.

65

Pleiades Revisited

I'm going into a forest. It's raining and there's a spider web. I shrank down so that I can see the spider web up close. I can see water dripping off it. The spider is very large right now. I don't think it can see me. A bug landed; there's a vibration on the spider web. In a split second the spider got it and wrapped it up. Now I'm back to my normal size in the forest.

What are you experiencing?

I realize that it's not our forest; it's on Pleiades. I'm coming into the city that I was in last time and going into the same concert hall. There's a show going on today and it's totally filled up with the most serene, delighted-looking Pleiadians. I can hear music, but it's completely dark in here. The stage is dark and they're listening to the music in the dark. It makes you focus just on the music. It's very engaging. Different kinds of vibrational music create feelings in me and pleasant emotions.

What else are you experiencing now?

I'm just sitting in the dark. I'm going back outside. The weather is similar to the last time I came. There are Pleiadians doing different activities, enjoying each other's company, talking, meditating. Little Pleiadians are playing an imaginary game, like chasing each other and pretending they're animals. These young Pleiadians — five or six years of our age — are just playing make believe. It's really cute.

There's a Farmers Market of sorts. There are different root vegetables and greens that they're sharing with each other in the community. They look like garlic, turnips and yams, similar kinds of food like that. They also have vegetables similar to our carrots and radishes. Everybody is so happy, so comfortable, there's no negativity.

Do they know that you're there?

Not today. I'm not really making myself known today. I'm just observing.

What are you experiencing now?

I'm just walking around. I'm watching the Pleiadians.

What are you observing?

A lot of chatting, a lot of talking, with kids playing around. It's a very close-knit community. Everybody knows each other and is comfortable with each other. I don't feel that there's anything to be worried about. There's no crime and there's nothing to be upset about. They're all comfortable and happy with each other. There's no conflict. At the market they were all sharing each other's food. They didn't have to buy it; they were just sharing it. They worked on it and wanted to share it; they are proud of their produce. They wanted the others to enjoy it too.

There's a big lake. Their sun is setting. I can see a couple of different moons, just dimly. The sky is yellow-orange. There are some Pleiadians meditating next to the lake. There's a group of them sharing each other's energy.

What are you experiencing now?

I'm sitting down next to the meditating Pleiadians. I'm picking up their energy and experiencing it. It's really phenomenal energy. When they meditate, there are people all around them, an active community, but they go so deep that it doesn't affect them. They're just so into their meditation.

Human Brain

I'm starting off in a human brain. I can see the different synapses connecting in different parts of the brain. It's really active.

Is it anyone's brain in particular or just a brain in general?

Maybe mine, or just one in general. I zoom around. I can feel activity in my own brain. I feel it all over my head, like I'm wearing a baseball cap.

Central America

I'm going into a wormhole now. I'm experiencing the colors going by really fast. I get off in a cavern. There are different minerals all over the walls. There are different crystals and colors and minerals in this cavern. I'm just experimenting with my third eye.

Where is this cavern?

It's here on the planet somewhere. It's in Central America. It's a big hall. I feel like I could yell and hear my name echo back. Light goes on for a while. Many of the walls are covered in minerals. Some of them are smooth material. I touch it; it's really smooth rock. I come out of the cavern.

There is a huge crystal-like, bright blue lake — a body of water. It's really blue, very pretty. It's somewhere in Central America. It's really quite beautiful. I'm just looking around now. I'm experiencing the jungle. I can hear all the jungle noises: monkeys, birds, and insects.

Mars

I'm in the wormhole and getting off on Mars. I'm in this dimension, though, the astral dimension. I can tell that it's really cold and rocky and darker than Earth. It has a dry, cold feeling.

The Andes

I come back into the wormhole now. I'm going to my spot up in the Andes. I haven't been here in a while. The air is really crisp — real nice, very pleasant. I'm just going to lay out here for a moment.

Water World

I'm back in the wormhole. I can create wherever I want, if I want to go somewhere.

Do you know where you're going or are you just going to end up somewhere?

I can create it if I want to. I'm going back in time. I'm going to Atlantis. I'm on the shore. There are massive ships on the water and they've got big sails, but they aren't like sailboats or sail ships. They're huge and look like ancient Greek ships, but they're different. There are different buildings around me, unusual structures and huge pyramids. It's all built on the water. There's water all around, maybe like Venice. They use little boats to get to different places. It has a very unique feeling. The buildings are very interesting.

What does that mean?

They're futuristic but in the past. They're all built on the water. Some of them are like pyramids coming up. I don't know what they're made of, types of stone I guess, different types of minerals and crystals. There are lots of crystals, a lot of crystal energy. They utilize the water everywhere, and solar energy as well. It's very interesting.

Ascended Masters' Retreat

There was an elevator in the field today. I got in it and went up into the heavens and got off in a big golden room with a golden hallway. It goes on for quite a while with golden trim and violet accents. It's a huge hallway. I could probably yell out and hear my name echo back. There are pictures on the wall of different ascended masters. They seem alive. They're pictures, but they're moving and smiling and kind of alive.

Which ascended masters do you see? Can you go up to the pictures and communicate with the ascended masters?

There's Saint Germain, Kuthumi, Master Jesus, and Serapis Bey. I see Djwal Kuhl, Lady Madonna, and more. I can talk to them, but they want me to keep walking. They want me to keep going to the end of the hallway. It opens up into a huge ballroom. There are stairs that wind around. They go back and forth. They go down to another level. It's a big room with a huge dome on top of the ceiling with different artwork, with artwork of angels. It's really beautiful. There are gold-plated walls and a type of ancient architecture.

Did you say gold-plated?

Gold-covered walls. There are big columns in the corners also covered in gold. There is purple trim in between, next to the columns and throughout the architecture.

Where is this place? Do you have any sense or any idea where you are? Is this on the Earth, in the Earth, or in some celestial region?

I took an elevator up to it. It's celestial.

Where do you imagine it is?

The heavens of some sort, wherever that is.

What else would the ascended masters like you for you to experience while you're there?

> There's a pool at the bottom of the stairs in this big room. It's not very big, just a little stone bath. I'm going to lie in it. I can float on top of the water and stare right up at the huge ceiling, the huge dome. I'm feeling rejuvenated and can feel the energy of all the amazing people, all the masters, that have been here before. I'm just floating right on top of this warm water.

> As I lie here, there's a carbon copy of me being made and my outline gets up. There's an outline of me now, like a shadow, not in a dark sense, but like a shadow copy of me. It spread out. It spread its hands and legs out and floated up through the ceiling. It's going through the dome. It's going out into the universe. I'm just going to follow it; the other part is just going to stay and lay on the bath.

> This outline of me went up into the universe and we're jetting around. It can create whatever it wants. It's creating a grid on the universe again, but this one is vertical. I guess it's vertical; I don't really know. It climbs up the grid and can alter it and change it, make it wavy. It can climb and do whatever it wants. It's really weird. It's just an outline of me. There's no face or anything. It's just an outline figure, but it has my energy. It's dancing on this grid in the universe. The grid is really big, so it takes up a lot of space. My outline can go places really quickly in the universe on this grid. I feel like I can travel past Saturn very quickly on this grid. Saturn is about the size of a basketball compared to the grid.

What are you experiencing now?

> We — me and the shadow figure of me — are going to stop at a planet. It's a planet of light and color. It has bright lights and rainbows and colors all over the place shooting off in every direction. Light is sparking everywhere. It's just shooting off in every direction, like fireworks, all over this planet. It has colors zooming around. There are lots of prisms and crystals that alter the light and create new light or create multiples of light. Light shoots into them and breaks off into more light.

Is your outline experiencing this while another part of you is observing your outline on this colorful planet?

Yes, I'm with my outline and I'm also still back in the bathtub.

And you're also with me back on the Earth. So there are at least three or four of you right now. (Laughter) Well, I've read about people who are able to manifest different parts of themselves elsewhere on the planet or in different parts of the universe simultaneously.

Yes. It's really very cool and I'm getting rejuvenated in the bathtub. It's such pure energy in this beautiful, golden room where I'm welcome to join anytime. I think they hold huge meetings here — important meetings about helping the whole universe. It's like a retreat of sorts, a rejuvenation retreat, and it's just magnificent. This is where they come together with ideas, help each other, help humanity, and help others.

I wonder if this place has a name.

I don't know. My outline has come back and my chakras are floating just above me. I pull them in one at a time and get out of the bath. There's an elixir for me.

What are you experiencing?

I drink the elixir. It shot through me very quickly. It was energy and rejuvenation. I felt it right away. I felt a little dizzy and then I came back. I'm back on the Earth now. I'm back in the field and I'm going to come back now.

Conversation after Retreat

How do you feel? What was that like?

That was a really cool experience.

Does it feel special?

Yes, it feels really special. What do you think about it all?

I think it's phenomenal. What was the elixir like? Was it there when you got out of the bath or did somebody hand it to you?

No, it was there when I got out of the bath. It was a cream-colored, thick elixir. It wasn't clear, it was thick.

What was it in?

It was in a glass. I drank it and felt energy, but I also felt dizzy, a little bit loopy. Then I woke up back on the Earth. I recall feeling rejuvenated like it was healing me, helping me.

How did you feel getting started on today's meditation?

It was fine. It was good.

What happened when you went to the field?

There was a little elevator waiting for me.

What did it look like?

It was about eight feet tall. It was probably a couple feet across. It was just a little one-person box.

How did you get in?

It was open on the one side. It had three sides and was also golden. There were a few columns. I went in and it took me up to a cloud or heaven or something. I don't know. It felt like the heavens. I got off and it turned into this big hall. It was a very long hall. It went on forever. Then, toward the end of the hall, there were big posters or pictures of the ascended masters.

The hall was decked in gold and violet?

Gold and violet. It was gold, tinged in violet, with a huge ceiling. I looked at it, started to reach the other end, and there were pictures of different ascended masters. They were lifelike.

Were they three-dimensional?

They were two-dimensional, but lifelike.

Did the pictures talk?

They could, I think, but they didn't.

Did they watch you as you traveled down the hallway? (Laughter)

Yes, but it wasn't creepy. (Laughter) They were warm and welcoming, not creepy.

Did you go up to them?

I went up to Saint Germain.

How did you know the others?

There were some nearby. I didn't look up at all of them. There were a lot of them.

So you went up to a few of them?

Yes. There was Saint Germain and Jesus and Kuthumi and Djwal Kuhl.

You also mentioned Lady Madonna and Serapis Bey.

Oh, yes. They wanted me to continue through the door.

There was a door at the end?

Yes.

You went through the door into a big meeting room?

Yes, kind of. This big room, like a ballroom, had a huge dome at the top with artwork of angels on it. The room was really pretty. It was gold with violet trim and big columns in the corners. It wasn't really ancient architecture. There was a path that wound around down to a bottom level. I was on the top level and it was the way to get down. It zigzagged back and forth.

You knew to do that?

I guess. Yes, I did that. So I went down there and there was a stone bath. It was not very big, just a pool for a bath. It was made of a golden stone. I got into the bath and laid out, just floated there on the water. Then my outline got up. It climbed out of me. (Laughs)

You watched it from the bath? You watched it as it left you?

Yes, I watched it leaving. It just climbed out of me, spread its arms and legs, and then it floated up.

It floated up through the ceiling?

It went up. It just floated up to the ceiling and then through the ceiling.

And you followed it?

Yes, I was able to be in both places. I could focus my energy and my consciousness in any spot that I wanted to. So I went out into the universe. I floated up through the ceiling and I went up to the sky and just kept going up. I went up until it was the universe. Then, my outline created the mixed grid or whatever it was. It could alter the grid and make it do whatever it wanted. It could spread it out or up.

It was moving its hands and making the grid shift?

Yes, exactly. And then it spread out.

Moving things around?

Yes.

So, were you experiencing yourself as the outline or were you experiencing yourself as the being floating on the pool?

I was both, I suppose. I feel like I moved both. So I did that. The outline made the grid grow. It grew and I could see the planets. The planets were all small because it made the grid spread out to go across the universe much quicker. So I went to that planet. There was light zooming around, sparking everywhere and shooting in every direction.

What do you think that was?

A light planet.

It had a lot of colors?

Yes, it had prisms and crystals. The light would shoot into the prisms and divide into a bunch of different colors and shoot off. It was moving quickly. All this light was moving really fast and then my outline came back to me. We came back, the outline and me, and it moved back into me. Then we got up and there was the elixir.

You didn't notice the elixir until you got out of the bath?

Yes, I don't think it was there before.

Did you drink the whole thing? How much was in there?

A decent amount. I drank it. It wasn't really like liquid. I mean, I guess it was liquid, but it didn't feel like liquid.

Perhaps it was liquid energy or something like that.

Yes.

What did you feel?

In the pool, I felt like I was rejuvenating in the bathtub.

Did you feel that it was time to come back?

Yes, I felt like it was time.

You had your experience?

I felt like it was a quick experience, but it was an appropriate experience and not to overdo it.

What do you think that was all about?

I don't know. What do you think?

I'm not sure. You went someplace where the ascended masters congregate. I don't know what to make of it. It sounds promising for your work. I don't think the ascended masters would pay so much attention to somebody if they didn't feel that they had important work to do. It seems like an experience that you should feel honored to have had. Do you feel like that?

Yes, definitely.

Apparently you are, and are not, in control of these experiences. To some degree you have no control over, or don't seem to have conscious control over, which experiences you will have. You had no idea that when you went into the field today that there would be an elevator there. And then you had this whole experience. Yet part of you is able to will things while you're in that state.

Yes.

So it seems to be a combination of the guides guiding things, placing imagery in your mind's eye, and you being able to choose some of the experiences. It's still hard to understand if it's just imaginary or if it's something else, what we think of as images in your mind versus you actually being in some other location, in some other dimension.

Yes, I don't know. I don't know where that line is anymore.

It's very interesting. Well, congratulations on that experience.

Thank you.

Follow-up with
Naor from LaZarus

*Good morning. It is I, Naor. May I answer some
questions today?*

Yes, hi Naor. I have some questions about Damiana's experience
yesterday. She traveled with her third eye to a beautiful, golden room
with several ascended masters. Where was that?

*That was one of the many private locations the
masters have upon your planet. That particular retreat
was located not far from the Himalayan Mountains.
The energy illuminating there was to help rejuvenate
and purify Damiana's channel as she moves further
along this path. She can visit there again whenever
she likes.*

To get there, Damiana traveled up in an elevator. She felt like she
was in some heavenly region. Are you saying the retreat was actually
located somewhere on the Earth?

*It's off the Earth, located above your Himalayas,
in another dimension just outside Earth's atmosphere.*

Was the elevator a visual tool that Damiana used to get there or that
the ascended masters used to bring her there? How does that work?

*Indeed, it was relatable to humans. So, through
the power of thought and imagination — a combination of Damiana's and the masters' intentions — the
elevator was conceived as a tool to bring her there.*

Once inside the retreat, Damiana saw pictures of ascended masters
on the wall, but they seemed to be alive. Please talk about that.

In other dimensions there are no limitations. While many of the masters were not physically present at the time, they left part of themselves there to greet Damiana and make her feel safe in their retreat in the sky.

Damiana floated on a rejuvenating pool of water. What was that?

This was energy to help open up and clear her vessel, helping along this path, giving her energy and confidence within the channel. She can go there whenever she likes to regain energy and confidence.

An outline or copy of Damiana left her body that was floating on the water and it traveled elsewhere in the universe. What was that about?

This was more experimentation with Damiana's will and third eye, as well as one of the non-limitations of these other worlds where she can stay and rejuvenate and go exploring at the same time.

Damiana's copy traveled to a planet of crystals and prisms with bright lights and colors shooting out in all directions. What was that planet?

That was one of many planets of light — light in its purest form enjoying just being as it illuminated around the planet and duplicated itself through prisms and crystals. There are many planets throughout the universe where light exists within itself. Some of them are similar to that one and others are very different. She can see more in the future.

When Damiana's copy returned to her body that was floating in the bath, she noticed that her chakras were floating just above her. She pulled them in one at a time. What was happening there?

They were rejuvenated. The energy within them was balanced and she herself had been balanced. So she was able to observe it in this world, bring them in, feel the balance, and get out of the bath.

When Damiana came out of the rejuvenating bath there was an elixir waiting for her. She drank it and felt high energy then quickly returned to Earth. What was the elixir and why did she return to her physical body so quickly?

> *Yesterday's experience for Damiana was to rejuve-*
> *nate her energy and clear her channel. While her*
> *experience was of the utmost benefit, the elixir was*
> *just finishing off the job and bringing her back to*
> *Earth, giving her a quick rejuvenation and returning*
> *her to the physical plane.*

When Damiana travels with her third eye, is she actually leaving her body or is that something different?

> *It's different. She's traveling with her third eye, but*
> *she is not leaving the body in the sense of an "out-of-*
> *body experience" or "near-death experience." She*
> *is physically here in presence while visiting other*
> *worlds through her mind's eye.*

I know that she's physically present, but it's still unclear to me whether her consciousness is actually leaving her physical body. Is that related to the third eye?

> *Indeed. Her consciousness is viewing other worlds*
> *through her third eye and visiting in that sense. In a*
> *way, she is bringing those worlds here to her con-*
> *sciousness instead of the other way around.*

When Damiana travels with her third eye, for example when she visited Pleiades, she seems to have some sort of a physical or etheric body that she brings with her. Can you talk about that?

> *Indeed. She does create herself into an ethereal*
> *body, but this is only for experiential purposes. And,*
> *again, she's bringing these worlds to her, not the other*
> *way around.*

Is it possible for her to go *there*? I don't understand. It seemed as though she was actually on Pleiades.

Yes. She is experiencing these planets and these worlds, but she is bringing them to her third eye. She is experiencing them through a clairvoyant vision. So she is truly experiencing them, but she is creating them here. It's very confusing, I know. As Damiana develops this gift and continues experimenting and using her third eye, these concepts will become more clear.

I have some more questions about the etheric body. Do humans have a non-physical, etheric body?

Yes, however many of the humans have forgotten about it. In your dreams each and every night, your etheric body turns to the astral world and explores. This etheric body is very real. You can consciously separate them during meditations as well.

What is the purpose of the etheric body?

The etheric body is your connection to the astral world and the universe so you are not stuck in this physical plane through your whole physical existence. There is still that connection to the etheric world which you came from. This is why sleep is so important for humans. It's important to make those connections at night and go back to your etheric world.

Is the etheric body related to the third eye?

It can be, but in a different way. In your dreams you travel in your etheric body, and your third eye is connected as well. When Damiana travels with her third eye, she creates her etheric body and places it in these worlds.

Do you have anything else you'd like to share with us before we end today's session?

Thank you. The pleasure is always mine.

Isis

I'm in Egypt listening to a sermon or a talk. Many people are gathered around listening.

> *I am Isis. We are redefining humanity. You are all creators and can redefine and create daily. Shed the cloak of the past, illuminating the golden aura of a brand new day. Go forth and resonate your golden energy. Share your sacred selves within the ever-growing Garden of Paradise that is created upon this planet. Each and every one of you has the power within. Behold this power! Never forget the energy, compassion and love of your brothers and sisters.*

This is a gathering of a secret society. I'm listening to this. We're underneath one of the pyramids, a secret compartment down underneath. There's a huge hallway with big, torch candles illuminating all around this underground compartment.

Do you have any idea of the time period?

I feel like it's before the birth of Jesus. It's a secret society within Egypt and these people were chosen. It's undermining the current pharaoh. He's not aware of these secret meetings. They are bringing spiritual power to the underclass that live here in Egypt at the time.

Who are the people that are listening to Isis?

I feel that they are light workers of the time.

Can you describe Isis?

She has strong energy, indigo or dark blue energy. She has an obvious presence but it's non-physical.

Atlantis

I am coming down from the universe and going to Atlantis again. I land on a boat this time. It's going through these big gates that keep the ocean water separate from the local water. I'm coming in and there are massive stone rocks that curve around a huge structure made of stone. It's covered in moss. There are glass pyramids around as well. I climb up these stairs. I can start to see more of Atlantis because I'm getting higher. I start to see an overview of it.

Did you come in on a boat from the ocean to land? Is this some sort of a docking area?

Docking, it's not really land. There is water all around the structures, but I got off onto this structure made of rock. It's really thick rock that's been carved into a structure and it curves around. This stairway goes up the structure really high and I can start to see more of Atlantis as I go higher. I can see glass pyramids, crystal domes, and more of these buildings carved out of rock. A lot of them are covered in moss. There is plant life growing within them as well.

It's really muggy and misty. The clouds hang low. It's an ancient city coming up through the clouds. I can see electricity shooting off in between certain structures. It reminds me of Tesla coils or something like that. This is like a beautiful lighthouse or bell tower that I'm on. These stairs curve around too, spiraling up to the very top. I can look far off into the city. When I go the other way, I can look off into the ocean. There are massive boats out there. There are dolphins jumping. It's an ocean city; it's crazy! There are statues carved out of stone. There is a big statue of Poseidon, with different ocean beings — half animal, half human-ish beings, or extraterrestrial even. Statues also surround this massive city.

Is this actually Atlantis or is this a city on Atlantis?

I think this is what Edgar Cayce described as Poseidia, one of the main capitals of Atlantis. I think there are more islands going out. When I look out to the ocean, I can see far off. I can see some lights and electricity. I think this is one of the main cities in Atlantis. It's incredible. It's really beautiful.

Do you see any Atlanteans?

I think the city is empty right now, between civilizations. Or maybe the people are just not where I am right now. I can see three moons, though. They're crescent and really big. I feel like they're closer to the planet than the Moon is today. They're really close and remind me of the Cheshire cat. They curve all the way around, all three of them.

I wonder what these moons are since we have only one moon today.

There's one that's bigger than the other two.

Buddhist Retreat

There's a beautiful bird, perhaps a pheasant, with golden feathers and black stripes on its wings. It glistens under the Sun's rays. I can really view the Sun today, each individual ray. A vibrational pattern jolts back and forth, layering on top of itself. I'm going to follow the bird.

I touch down in Thailand, or somewhere nearby. There's a Buddhist statue all in gold. It's really tall. It has three eyes, including its third eye. One hand is up and the other is on its legs in a lotus position. The Buddhist temple is a deep red, maroon, with stone tile and little meditation pillows to sit on around the room. I'm at a fountain or a pool on the other side of the Buddha. The coins tossed in are shimmering out. I can see the vibrations again.

The vibrations of the Sun's rays?

Of the coins in the water, light shining off them. It radiates. Everything is radiating.

Is anybody present?

The bird is still here. The room is empty right now.

Do you know what kind of bird it is?

It's big, the size of a peacock, but it looks like a pheasant or a quail. It has gold, shiny feathers, black stripes on its wings, and black eyeliner.

Did the bird take you here to meditate?

Maybe. It's a very nice meditation room. So, yes, perhaps I should meditate here with the giant Buddha.

Do you know what country this is?

I think Thailand or Bali, perhaps even China; I don't know. It's somewhat tropical, near the equator. There's something very humble about the room. Although it's extremely radiant and glamorous, there's a humble feeling too.

Is this another retreat of some sort? Who meditates here?

I feel like it's on the Earth and people can go here in physical form — a Buddhist retreat on Earth. It has really nice energy, but I don't feel like it's an ascended master retreat, per se. I feel their energy, but not in the same way that I did in the sky.

Well, maybe it's a Buddhist retreat.

Yes. I feel like you would physically go here, though. I feel like we can visit Thailand and go here in our physical bodies.

What else are you being guided to see or do while you're there?

I'm just looking around right now. The bird is on the shoulder of the Buddha. It's a really big Buddha. It takes over the room. It's not a huge room; it's very nice though. I'm going to sit down and meditate for a moment and then I'm going to move on.

I'll meditate with you here.

Time Travel

I came out of my meditation and there was smoky-blue indigo washing over me. Then I went backward on a timeline. It stopped at different points in history, from the English coming over to America in boats, to Native Americans, and it kept on going back. I came back to the cavemen and these interesting cave drawings. There were Pleiadians watching them, observing them from afar, like a field study. I was wondering if the cavemen were mutants from Atlantis and how it all fits in with Darwin's theory, or whether that was even before Atlantis or something that came out of Atlantis because of the flood that created new life forms. I wondered about the mutants that were left there. The Pleiadians are just watching the cavemen.

The smoky-blue indigo came back. It's just cloudy and smoky, much like the very first time with my third eye when I couldn't focus. There was a lot of this, these clouds that come at me, this smokiness. It's not overwhelming like the first time. It's just this astral world. It stopped now, but it was happening the whole time that I was telling that story.

Now I'm looking up at the night sky. The constellations are really clear. The stars are really bright. It's a perfectly clear night. It's really beautiful. I'm within it.

Fuzzy Beings

I went up into the universe. I stopped on a planet and there are fuzzy little beings here. They are really short, like one-and-a-half feet tall, and they have a little civilization. All of the fuzzy little beings look the same, to me at least.

Where are you now? What are you experiencing?

I zoomed out from this planet to get a better look at it. It's just massive, the universe.

Africa

What are you experiencing now?

I'm going somewhere else now, to the plains of Africa. There's a herd of wildebeest and I see some elephants, just a couple of them, and some meerkats. It's really dry here — dry plains. The dirt's all broken up. They haven't had rain in a while. There's a little dung beetle pushing dirt along. I'm just watching the animals here and experiencing the heat.

Is this in present time or during some historical period?

Present time, maybe. I just wanted to see if I could go here. There's a little temple now. [Breathes deeply] I'm breathing in the air, just feeling the energy, feeling an ancient energy.

Where is this temple?

It's in the sky.

Is this another retreat of the ascended masters?

Yes, maybe. It has really good energy with an ancient smell to it. I'm floating inside the temple. It's made of marble, or something like that.

Third Eye Strain

See if you can come back to this room and observe us meditating.

I'm here, I think.

What are you experiencing now?

I am surrounded by swirling smoke again. Sometimes figures come out of it, but just the outlines. Sometimes I'll see extra-terrestrial outlines, Buddhist outlines, or third eye outlines, or maybe my own outline.

Can you blow the smoke away and create clarity?

There's a lot of strain on my third eye. I can feel it working really hard.

What's causing the strain?

I don't know, I'm just using my third eye. I can feel it like a muscle that you're using, like holding a weight and eventually you start to feel it.

Maybe the more that you exercise it the easier it'll become.

Yes. There's a bug on my leg.

I removed the bug.

Thank you. The vibrations create patterns that move around. I can see them and the energy being transferred.

Looking Ahead

See if you can travel into your future by two or three years.

I can see myself. I'm in front of a large group of people in a conference room, holding a big talk with one of the extraterrestrials speaking through me. I'm sitting up and moving my hands when I talk and it's much more connected than it is now. My eyes are still closed. The people in the room are all listening very eagerly. They're very excited, the energy is very exciting.

What is the extraterrestrial saying?

It's discussing with them how manifestation works, explaining how they can achieve the lives they want. I think the extraterrestrial is probably Adam.

What are you experiencing now?

I was watching the patterns. I'm going to come back. My third eye is really hurting.

Past Lives

I'm in a crystal room. There are different types of quartz around me — amethyst, rose, smoky — jutting out of the walls. I'm sitting cross-legged with candles surrounding me. There are three people sitting in front, just slightly below me. I'm connecting with other worlds, doing readings for them. They came to me. I think that I live here in this crystal cave. They're very important people. It's in Atlantis and they're royalty; they came to me to help them make difficult decisions about how to rule the land. I go into a trance state and a being comes in. It's warning them that they need to change the way that they're ruling because it will destroy them. They need to put more emphasis on sharing, and loving the people of their kingdom.

Is there anything else that is important for you to know or remember from this experience?

The connection that I had in this life is so much more direct and pure. I can reach that point again.

Who were the entities that came through you? Whom did you work with during that period?

I worked directly with the Creator, with higher Self connected with everything. Only the purest and highest truths would come through me.

What did you do to achieve such a pure connection so that the trance state could take place?

I dedicated my life to working for this higher connection. I spent much of my life on this planet in this world, alone in this cave connecting to the higher spirits, going within for hours out of the day, creating this connection for much of my waking life. I heard voices when I was a child, so I had been working at it since I was very young.

What were you called or known by?

They called me the Seer. I was very mysterious to the people in the town. Only the strongest and bravest of heart would make the journey to come see me. But those who came would have life-changing experiences. They were called to me.

How did you support yourself? Did they pay you? How did you live? How did you survive?

The spirits kept me alive. I don't think I ate physical food. I just spent my time in this cave, most of the time in other worlds. I didn't ask for payment.

There must have been a way that you ate.

I don't think so. I don't think I ate. I think I lived off the connection.

What are you experiencing now?

I'm a little boy on a different planet. There's light illuminating down on the planet. My family is making dinner. Outside, the family is preparing the table. There's a light that shines down on us. It's different from the Sun. I'm extraterrestrial and ethereal looking. I have golden skin, no hair. I can have a third eye if I want to, but I don't have to. I have this quality about me that's very serene. The area looks almost tribal in nature. My family's home is kind of like a hut. I'm probably around eight years old. It's such a different planet. I'm wearing a necklace with a diamond and a crystal. It glows and radiates light. I'm letting the light bounce around me. I'm feeling the heat from it; it feels warm.

Do you know where this planet is, or what type of extraterrestrial you are?

I think it's in the fifth dimension. I'm a different kind of extra-terrestrial, a Light Being extraterrestrial. Our species has mastered going back and forth between ethereal existence and physical existence. We aren't tied down to our physical bodies, so we can travel if we wish to.

My family prepared dinner, all different types of roots and vegetables. There's no meat and the water is fizzy, different from ours. It gives you a kind of bubbly energy when you drink it. I have three sisters, two of whom are older than me; one is younger. My parents are celebrating something like a summer solstice. The energy is really high and bright.

Do you know the time period?

I think it's in the past, maybe 4,000 years ago in humanity's time. We don't have time on this planet. After dinner I go outside and the light has ducked behind the planet. It's still pretty bright. I can start to see some of the stars. They're much closer to us than Earth's distance to the stars. They're like big orbs in the sky swirling around.

We're gathering with others for the show. There's going to be a show tonight in the sky. There will be different orbs illuminating, creating tones, creating music that is different from ours. The energy of each orb at a distance from our planet vibrates off of our planet and boomerangs back creating these echoes, creating the sounds. Some of the beings dance and some of them sing along. It's a joyous festival for some of them. Others just watch. It's very unique.

What are you experiencing now?

I'm on my grid overseeing the universe. I can throw vibrations out into different areas. I can draw the Earth in and send positive vibrations to it. Some people feel them, others are too busy with their daily lives; they don't notice them. I can bring in other planets too and do the same. I can jet across the universe. I'm ethereal. I don't really have a body. I can create light, sound, movement, vibration, color, matter, energy. I can create my own planet if I want to, but mostly I like to send positive energy toward planets. It ripples and gathers on the planet, but some of it just keeps going out into the universe forever.

Do you work with anybody or do you work by yourself?

I work with everybody. I recognize the universal connection that I have, and I have everyone's energy with me. I manipulate the negative energy back into positive energy. I take it in like a tree. I take in the bad energy and emit positive energy. I'm connected with the plants. I'm connected with the extraterrestrials, humanity, animals, down to the smallest microorganism. I'm connected to star clusters, star planets, Light beings, gas beings, vapor beings, to all types of beings in different dimensions and different worlds. Some of them developed negative ways and some of them are more enlightened. They all share my energy.

I can pull the Pleiadian planets in near me and watch them. Everything emits a vibration and a color. I'm observing. I see where there are ailments on the planets. Sometimes I'll send vibrations to a planet and some of the beings on that planet can feel those vibrations, but they do the opposite of me and manipulate them into negative vibrations, which they send out on their own planet. I can see this happening on the Earth in the Middle East but that's out of my control.

What are you experiencing now?

There's a little, old man. He'll speak in a minute.

> *Greetings, I have worked with Damiana through many lifetimes. We are giving samples of some of her past lives, but there is much more in Damiana's history that we are keeping locked up for the time being. As Damiana develops in this lifetime, she will release and unlock more of her history for herself. She is a very special soul for your planet at this time and it is of the utmost importance that you continue working, developing, and re-manifesting her potential, for there is so much more that she has to bring to the table. Continue daily with this practice and all shall develop as she set forth for herself in this lifetime.*

Damiana, is there anything else that you'd like to share or are you ready to return?

I'm ready to return.

Inner Space

Colorful Horses

I'm going to the field. It has really bright colors — bright orange, yellow, green, blue, and purple. As I walk further into the field, different colors come down on me. I can feel them. They each have different energy. There are also horses that are different colors, mostly blue and purple horses. They're running wild around here on this back area of the field that I've never been to. They trot upwards toward the sky creating an invisible, spiral staircase into the heavens. I go up through the rainbow sky into the cosmos, between the dark night and the horizon where it's real bright with pretty colors from a sunset or a sunrise. There are bright pinks and purples and oranges before you get to the deep, dark blue with some of the first or last stars becoming visible. I'm just taking it all in.

South America

What are you experiencing now?

I'm on planet Earth, perhaps in South America or Central America. It's humid. There are cliffs with caves in them. There's a very thin rope bridge going across. It doesn't look very stable. There are cliffs going down into the valley. On the cliffs there are cave dwellings. I think these are ancient sites. They've been covered up with plant life. It has grown over a lot of the entrances and architecture so they're hard to see. An ancient tribe used to live here. I just went into a cave. I have to get down on all fours and crawl, because the further you go in, it becomes very tight. It barely fits around me. It's just a little crawl space. There's a small tunnel going back into the Earth, into this cliff. It starts to open up. There are some pools back here. Water is dripping into a small pool. It's starting to open up to big rooms, secret locations where ancient tribes met or lived.

Why are you experiencing this?

I'm just experimenting with my third eye because I haven't in a while.

Yes, but why did you end up here? You didn't even know about this place yet you came to it. What is higher spirit trying to share with you about these caves?

I don't know. A lot of times when I travel, my third eye just starts seeing things. I don't know why I have these experiences. Sometimes I just see a lot of colors and patterns. Waves of color come down on me. Bright colors shoot all around me. Vibrations of color are around us all the time. We just aren't at a high enough frequency yet to realize this. There are colors and sounds and all sorts of things that we haven't even experienced. They're beyond our comprehension. Sometimes the animals can see and hear and feel them. We can pick up on them, though, if we pay attention. But these are just small glimpses of them, not the whole experience.

I climbed up through a different exit from the cave. There are built-in steps or notches on the wall. I climbed all the way up the steps to a sky light. I'm just peeking through a tiny hole. Water gathers at the bottom of it. It comes through the hole when it rains. I'm now in a mossy, green area. There are plants everywhere. Some of the plants are like Venus Fly Traps. There are different kinds of interesting plants, very exotic plants, and some flowers that I've never seen before. There are huge, really bright flowers — one flower is about 18 inches across and eight inches deep — with beautiful colors. They're very attractive.

(Damiana breathes deeply several times.) I'm gathering energy from all the plant life and everything around me. I'm picking up on the energy like a tornado and utilizing it within me, bringing it in, mixing it with my energy. I can see it happening, I can see myself taking in the energy, but I also share mine so the plants aren't destroyed. We share this nice exchange of energy. I can see the energy coming into me. I can see the different colors and waves of energy.

Seahorses

What are you doing now?

I'm in a certain space now. There are things floating around. This is an astral area. There are giant seahorses and specks of light and dust and energy shooting about. I still see waves of energy and color. I'm just floating here experiencing it. These specks gather together. Some of them follow each other and become really thick and fuzzy. Some disperse to other places. A lot of them are like schools of fish where they travel together in a group or family. There are long ones that dart about by themselves. The seahorses are huge, bigger than me.

Are you in the water?

No. I'm in space. Not outer space, but an astral space.

Inner space?

Yes, inner space. I don't know why there are seahorses. I guess I just created them. They are very beautiful.

What are you experiencing now?

I'm just watching different things that are in this space. There are microorganisms of some sort, too. They have a jelly shape with frills coming off of them. They're interacting with other ones like them. These are just different organisms, I guess. They have different vibrations. Everything in the world — anything that you could imagine — could be here.

Is it an enclosed space or is it an open space?

It's open and wide. I suppose it could go on forever. It's a wide area, so anything is possible. It's a meeting ground, an in between space for matter, and lack of matter as well. It's not purgatory. It's a crossing over point between dimensions and worlds.

Black Hole

See if you can travel into the universe and find a black hole.

Do you want me to go in it?

That's up to you.

I went in it. It's a parallel universe. It's a mirror image of the same one that I just came from. I can go back and forth through this black wormhole. They've got planets here — and the same ones right here on the other side. I can come back and forth through the hole. The planets are the same but different in a lot of ways.

Cartoon Extraterrestrial

I'm coming back, but I saw a tall woman who was not proportional. She was very skinny, very tall, and had a really long neck. If you pushed her on either side, she would stretch out somehow. I don't know how to describe it.

Was she just in space?

I don't know. She was walking. She was cartoon-like but human looking as well. She had short, blond hair. She just came out of nowhere, thanked me and then disappeared.

I wonder who she was and why she thanked you.

I don't know. She's an extraterrestrial doing her work.

Changing Perspective

I can keep pushing out and growing. Everything keeps getting smaller and smaller. It's like pushing back in water, doing the backstroke. The same things come and go, getting smaller as I keep going, but nothing is changing. The further I get away, the closer they come back to me. It's very confusing. I feel like Alice in Wonderland. It just goes on forever, infinitely.

I'm back in the field and it's still colorful. I'm back in the colors. I'll just lay down for a moment.

Tesla Energy

There are planets spinning around, like a mobile of planets. It's kind of making me dizzy. I'm moving through them. I stopped on a planet with electricity shooting everywhere —lightning bolts and different forms of technology with electricity. The beings of this planet are utilizing a lightning and thunder storm that is occurring, using the energy from it to power their planet. This planet is kind of dark and dreary, maybe because of the storm. I'm not sure if this is constant weather on the planet, but it's very technological and built very much around this electricity from lightning that goes around the city. There are bridges connecting a lot of the cities, with water — big lakes and rivers — going through. They have paths (but not roads) and there are tubes beside the paths where we have our sidewalks. They can shoot through the tubes, I think, like the tubes at a drive-through bank, to get to different spots.

A lot of the city is underground. I travel down deep into the planet where they have these caverns of cities. I see lightning bolts striking between different connections down below, too. It's Tesla coil-like stuff, for the energy is being manipulated and worked with. They have this material, an iridescent-like glass, but it's stronger than glass. I can hit against it and it feels pretty strong, like steel, but it's not a type of metal at all.

What are you experiencing now?

There's a laboratory of some sort down in the city where this electricity is being manipulated and tampered with, with different magnetic coils going around the length of the room. It's a plant of some type.

Like an electric plant?

Yes, like a base. There's an elevator with a bunch of buttons. I go into it and go down first. It goes deeper into this planet and

I can hear water dripping. It's a see-through elevator. I can see the dirt of the planet and I go down deep into their ground. There's a sewage system down here — a sewer or irrigation system. I go back up. There are different levels and different areas with water flowing. There's a room with big windows; it's under the water. The lake's right up against it and you can look out into the water. There are creatures in it, prehistoric-looking sea creatures with huge jaws. There's music playing on this level, American-like music from the 1920s or 1930s. It's not English that's playing, but it has an upbeat kind of old sound to it. It reminds me of milkmen and husbands going off to war, and moms staying home, like the typical nuclear family with green grass and a white-picket fence, that kind of music.

I'm in the elevator going back up to the surface. It's still raining out here. Maybe I'll go up and look at the top of the lake. The water creatures are huge compared to me. Across the way there's an island jutting out above the water.

Do you see any beings on this planet?

No, not right now, although I can feel their energy down in the lab.

Singing Owls

I'm zooming through space in a corkscrew motion. I'm spinning and winding around, going straight in one direction, but turning around and around. I land in a forest with evergreens and really big trees. There are owls, lots of them all around me, different sizes and colors, brown, gray, black, and white, clucking and talking to each other. It's nighttime. I lay down and look up at the sky. There are a couple of moons, and stars. I feel like it's potentially on the planet Earth, but I'm not sure.

What are you experiencing now?

Colors in the sky, like the Northern Lights. There are waves of different colors streaming across the sky and the owls are singing to it. They sing a beautiful song that I have the honor of listening to as they perform with these lights. They don't do this for everyone. I'm very lucky.

Are you listening to the song?

Yes, it's so enchanting. The experience is really amazing.

Are they hooting or clucking? You described them as clucking.

That was before, when they were talking to each other. Now they're singing. It's different from hooting and clucking. It's a melody that they make with different tones. Combined, it makes a beautiful sound. I don't know the musical term for it.

A song?

They sing together, different tones. It creates images within images, mostly of nature — rivers, mushrooms, moss, night skies, sunsets and sunrises, rain hitting on water.

Maybe you're interpreting the tones the way that they're intended, as a beautiful song and a type of communication.

Yes, they're different things the owls are familiar with that they connect with on their nightly interactions. I'm thanking the owls. It was such an honor.

What are you experiencing now?

I'm coming back. My third eye hurts a bit.

Forbidden Gateway

There was a gateway. I got the sense that I wasn't allowed or supposed to go through it. It was forbidden, but I went through it anyway to see what it was like. It was beautiful energy with golden-white streams of light. I felt like the streams were people passing over and I wanted to check it out. It was beautiful, golden-white streams of light, a pop of energy.

A pop of energy?

When I passed through to the other side.

It was a stronger energy, a different energy?

Yes.

So, these were people that were dying and going to the other side? You weren't supposed to go there because you aren't dying, but since you are astral traveling, you could go there and check it out?

Yes.

Neon Cave Dwellers

I'm in a cave. I crawl on my hands and knees. There's a little stream, a little pool of water in the cave. I work with the water, trying to manipulate the energy out of it or to put my energy into it. I'm focusing, concentrating, on this water. I'm trying to see what I can manifest into this water. It's vibrating ever so slightly. I'm concentrating and not breaking concentration. It's really vibrating now, like there's an earthquake, but just in the water, in this little pond. I can pull the water up. I'm pulling it up, pulling it out of the pool. It takes really deep concentration, unbroken concentration, and if I break it just for a second it goes back to the beginning. I must stay very focused.

Sometimes I see things that are hard to describe, like colors and shapes. I wish there was a video camera in my head. Sometimes I perceive concepts that are beyond human understanding. I don't understand them or how to share them. I see a wheel, like an ancient Aztec or Mayan wheel with all sorts of different carvings in it, and different parts, like a center that turns one way and then another part that turns a different way.

I go further into the cave. I crawl on my hands and knees and get to a point where I can let go. It's like coming through this peephole into a ceiling. This area opens up into a really tall ceiling. There are stalactites and ice and water dripping in the distance. There's a peephole going straight up. The energy here is really fantastic, like a sacred site. Things happened here in the past. The energy I'm picking up is really wonderful, a vortex area, I guess. There are rays of color, vibrations, going up and out through this peephole: ultraviolet and green and orange, vibrating and then they go up. There is a ring of color around me, then it goes up and out, a whole, colored light. They can change into bars, shapes, and mazes of color —vibrating strings and paths of color. Just a thin line of vibrating color, illuminated color, a glowing light source.

What are you experiencing now?

There are rows and rows of little colored beings. There are green and orange and yellow ones. They gather in a line. The orange ones are together and the green ones are together.

What are they?

Little beings. They're in lines that go on for quite a while. They are bright, neon colors. I head further through the cave on my hands and knees. It's getting foggy and a little muggy like a swamp. I'm crawling through water. I can't see very well because it's really foggy. The air has grown really thick. I'm by myself on the edge. If I step off, it goes really deep into a watery area that's the same temperature as me, so it's really weird. It doesn't feel like water. Something feels different because it's the same temperature as me. I don't know how far down it goes, or what kind of liquid it is, because it's not really water. The fog is developing from whatever kind of liquid this is. It's not made up of the same elements on the Earth.

What are you experiencing now?

I'm still in this foggy, swampy area of the cave, but it has opened up to the outside. It's dark outside. The fog is pretty high up but if I look through it, I can see out to the sky. There are stars and planets. It's different from Earth. There is a big cliff not very far from me. As I start to climb up the cliff, I look over at the fog which is covering a lot of this very foggy planet. As I come to the top of the cliff, I start to see the night sky much better. There's a spaceship going by. A UFO floated by.

Who's in it?

More of those little beings, but these ones are all black, no color to them. They seem more active than the colorful ones on the planet. They are very extraterrestrial. They don't seem to show much emotion or notice me at all. They're just busy doing whatever they need to do.

Cosmic Ribbons

Universal Math

I am seeing golden-yellow light streams — ribbons — and they're going off in different directions of the universe. I try to follow them. They take me to different facets of the universe. I go to one place where there are numbers shooting through the sky, tons of them. There are mathematical operations and figures that I don't recognize.

Do these numbers represent laws of the universe?

Maybe. They're shooting around like flying stars and it looks like a crazy math professor's blackboard, totally covered in numbers with different solutions and puzzles. They jet past me and just keep coming, more of them with huge operations. I recognize some of the mathematical symbols, but I don't recognize other symbols.

Why do you suppose you're seeing these?

I don't know. I followed one of the yellow ribbons and it took me to this part of the universe. It's like the makeup of the universe or the patterns that connect everything in the universe, how they relate to mathematics and physics, I guess. And they just keep coming; it's infinite.

Can you follow where the numbers are coming from? See if you can go to the source.

I don't think there's an end to it. I think it circles at some point, perhaps, or just continues infinitely. I don't think there is a source to it. It just keeps going. I don't want to say it's repeating itself because they're different, but I can keep going and it just continues.

Pastel Gases

I'm back to the yellow ribbon. I'm following it back to the swirls of yellow ribbons. I'm taking another yellow ribbon to a green planet. There are trees covering the planet. It's mossy, almost bouncy. It has some sort of spring to it. It's a different kind of plant life form. The trees are rather big and they have large nuts or seeds, much bigger than common nuts or seeds on Earth. They're about the size of a grapefruit, but in the shape of an eye. There are tears on either side.

I don't see any extraterrestrial, animal, or human life form, just the plant life. It's all green, bright green, really vivid green. The soft, spongy consistency reminds me of moss, if it were bouncy. I can see particles and gas in the air. They are different colors, very clear, but with color — light pinks and oranges and yellows. I assume it's some sort of gas. It swirls around in the sky, not too far off the planet. They are like pastel gases.

Do you have any idea where this planet is or why you're being given the opportunity to go there and visit?

It's in another dimension, perhaps a higher dimensional planet. I don't really know where it is in relationship to the Earth.

What are you experiencing now?

I'm just laying down on the bouncy, mossy floor. I'm watching the colors swirl around. They make different patterns — windmill patterns and funnel patterns.

The gases do this or the moss does this?

The gases; I'm laying on the moss looking upward.

Are these gases just part of the atmosphere?

Yes, I think so, but I can see them. They're clear pastel and move in patterns, then change to different frequencies, I guess. They're like waves, but different.

Apocalyptic Planet

See if you can follow another ribbon.

Okay. I followed another ribbon and it took me to a desolate planet. It's destroyed. There are fires and fireballs crashing around creating impact on the planet. It's apocalyptic-feeling, very dark.

Did beings ever exist on this planet?

Probably. I feel like they did, but there's nothing for miles except these fires and the fireballs shooting down, some of them hitting, some of them not.

Why is this planet being impacted? Is it being hit by meteors?

I guess. I don't know. They are big fireballs or meteors of some type. It feels like something that someone's imagination created. I don't know how else to describe it.

Is this the Earth's future or some other planet elsewhere?

It has a non-genuine feeling.

Perhaps you're experiencing someone else's imaginative creation.

Maybe, or a dream. I don't know.

No Limitations

I just pushed myself away from the ribbon. I'm backstroking through space, propelling myself farther. The ribbon is getting tiny.

Do you see any other souls out there?

Not right now, but they're around on their own journeys.

See if you can go to another dimension. See if you can travel to higher dimensions.

I don't have that limitation right now, so nothing is stopping me.

Swimming through Space

What else are you experiencing?

There are colors and lights in the sky that are like organisms, with paisley shapes going around in different colors, like pink teardrops with yellow and orange bulbs around them, with little squiggles drawn on them, things like that. They're all different shapes, but they seem to have some sort of life to them.

Can you travel to another planet?

I'm swimming through space. I come up to this blue planet with no structure to it. It all melts into itself like it doesn't begin and doesn't end; there's no shape or structure. It's just all together. I don't know how to describe it. It's like there's no backbone or anything to it or anything on it, or outlines — nothing defining one thing from another thing.

Does anything live on it?

There are little, black, big-headed things with small tails. They almost look like music notes or tadpoles or sperm. They are bouncing and dancing — the first things I've seen with any shape on this planet and they are jumping and dancing. They're moving together in a pattern, not so many of them, just a couple dozen.

Where are you now?

I'm swimming in the universe, just pushing myself through the universe, coming back down to my body. I'm back in my body, just back here, just breathing.

Are you ready to return?

In a couple of minutes.

Okay, bring yourself back when you're ready.

Highway to Heaven

I didn't know where to go, so I just focused on going to a place where other souls were. I am at a place with a somewhat smoky consistency. There are souls passing over from physical existence to non-physical existence. It's a stream of white light. You can see outlines a little bit as they come in.

Is it smoke or is it just streams of light?

There are streams of light coming through, but there's fogginess to it around me.

Are they people who recently died and are returning to the soul realm?

I think so, yes. There's a trail of them and it looks like they are all connected from their third eye. There's light through the white beam. There are figures with a light beam that shines through them connecting to the third eye area. They are heading up together. There are also ones heading the other way.

Are they only going in two directions?

They're going up and down from my viewpoint.

It sounds like Heaven and Hell.

No, I think they're going back onto Earth. They're reincarnating in the other direction.

Oh, that's interesting. Some of them are leaving and some of them are returning.

It's interesting because those that are going up are all connected, but the ones that are going down are by themselves.

It makes sense when we think about how alone we feel on the Earth. What are you experiencing?

To be honest, I'm emotional from it. Everybody thinks that you die alone but you don't. It's being born, coming to the Earth experience, that is lonely.

See if you can follow one of the souls that is about to reincarnate. See if you can watch as they do that.

There is a non-physical line between physical existence and non-physical existence. It's unknown to me even in this world. I don't know how to describe it. I can't really follow them.

Is that because it's private and off-limits to you?

I think so, at least at this time.

What about the ones that are dying? Can those be followed, the ones that are going back to the astral world?

They're going up. It's going on for a long time — thousands of them going up and they're all connected. Then it comes to a point and some of them break off and some of them stay together. It's just a world of white light. I don't know how else to describe it.

What are you trying to describe? What are you seeing?

Light, pure light.

Is this where they are going or who they are?

Both. It's just light. They're all heading toward the light. When they reach the light some of them stay connected from the third eye and others break away on their own. But they are still connected because this energy is all connected to the infinite power source that we're all connected to.

Can you go toward the light?

Yes, but not in the same way that they are connected to it.

What are you experiencing now?

I'm just watching. It's time to come back to my body now.

Lunar Worlds

Stairways and Doorways

I opened a door into the sky. It's on the Moon. Everything is white. There are stairways going everywhere, up and around. There are spiral ones, square ones, going up to different constructions built up around them. Everything's white. It's almost like an M.C. Escher painting the way these stairways keep going everywhere.

Is this on the Moon?

Yes. I'm going to open up doors. It looks like nothing is there, but you open the door and go through into a new room. It's very weird, very higher dimensional feeling. After climbing a lot of steps, there's just a doorframe. You step through it and it looks like you'll just fall into nothingness, like you're just going to drop off. But instead, once you go through, it's like going into a portal. They lead to other places altogether.

Are you going to enter one of the doors and see where it takes you?

In a moment.

Your third eye travels are like hallucinogenic trips.

There are little beings in astronaut-like suits. They're short, with big round heads. I don't know if their heads are round but they've got little helmets on. I don't know if they can breathe without their helmets.

You found these beings by going through one of the doors?

They're around. They're Moon-beings.

Can any of them communicate with you?

Not really. They're all moving quickly like they are in a rush to get somewhere.

Where are they going? Follow one of them. See where they're going.

He got into a little hovercraft. I'm zooming around following him. He's going outside the city, away from all of the steps. It's a suburb of sorts. He got out, parked his hovercraft and boarded a moving sidewalk. It's different from our moving sidewalks. It's built right into the ground and moving quicker than ours. It looks similar to our regular sidewalk but it's moving. Everything is still white. I see Moon-beings flying around in their hovercrafts and ones on the ground.

What dimension is this? Can you tell?

I don't know but it's higher than us.

I wonder why they have to wear astronaut suits.

I don't know. They might be shorter humans.

I wonder if they are from someplace else and just took up residence on this dimension on the Moon.

Maybe. They could be progressive humans. Perhaps in the future humans will learn how to breathe on the Moon. We're still on the sidewalk going past other little cities and whatnot. He has a little white briefcase. Everyone and everything looks the same. I don't see any pink or purple outfits. They're all wearing white and have little white briefcases. I haven't seen any animals.

I wonder if they don't have access to color and you're just perceiving it from their own perspective.

I don't know. I can look out into the sky. It's night time and there are stars. You can see some light color in the stars, like red giants or blue dwarfs. It's not very different than looking at the sky from the Earth. I can see the Earth. It looks like the Moon.

Ant People

See if you can travel to one of Jupiter's moons.

It's huge as I get closer, a giant rock with craters. It's beige in color and dusty. I'm pushing into the ground. Brown dust kicks up everywhere. And it's cold. I'm walking around on this desolate, dusty, cold moon.

See if there are any civilizations on this moon in another dimension.

I shrank down. I think it's a different dimension. There are tiny beings. They're very interesting, very tiny, not any bigger than our ants. There are whole cities, little barns and structures. They remind me of our ants; they have six arms (or legs) too. They're very busy running around. I can see little ones, children, playing in a playground with a little merry-go-round. There are little swings made out of wood. Everything looks like it's hand-crafted, mostly out of a wood-like material. It's funny because when I zoom out you can't even see them, just the dust. Then, when you go really close in you've got this whole little civilization with little playgrounds and barns and houses. I wonder if we have them on the Earth too?

Do they have any awareness of you?

No, they don't know anything about me. I think I would terrify them, destroy their whole world. I would be a god to them. Their whole world could fit on my pinky.

Would you be a god or a Godzilla?

Yes, probably Godzilla. Their whole world could fit on my pinky without any of them falling off.

How much space are they taking up?

(Laughs) When I zoom out you can't see them at all, it just goes back to the dust.

Are they little microbes?

They're people. They have four arms and two legs.

So they're like ant people? How do they walk? Are they upright?

(Chuckles) Yes. Hah.

What are their hands like? Do they have fingers or claws?

(Laughs) They have small hands. I don't think they have thumbs but four fingers on each hand.

No thumbs? How do they pick things up?

Their fingers have different joints. They're differently jointed, like a sloth. I think they can pick things up fine. All their fingers are opposable if that makes sense.

Their fingers are thumbs. (Laughs)

(Laughs) Yes.

What are they doing?

A lot of them are just living, going to work, gardening, and cutting down trees. Little kids are playing, running around. It's a little community without any technologies or metals. It has an ancient feeling, but they're happy and excited. They're doing their thing. I bet they think the world is flat, and to them it is.

Emerald Moon

Go to another moon.

I went to another moon. It's made of emeralds — green, like a marble with a cat's eye through it. It's emerald, a bright green marble in the sky. There are designs on the surface almost like crop circles printed into the structure of the moon.

What else do you see? Do you see any beings?

No. I'm going to come back. My visions aren't as vivid as they were at the beginning.

Revelations

I heard the beat of tribal drums off in the distance. I started seeing patterns. Then I met my tour guide. He was African, with paint on his face and body. He got down on one knee, welcoming me. Then, he transported us to the Congo. The drums were beating during my entire experience.

Zeus and the Ascended Masters

Suddenly I heard, "Up, up, up!" It was the ascended masters. I started to go up but I guess I wasn't going up fast enough because I heard Zeus bellow above everyone, "UP, UP, UP!" He pulled up the ground. Everything went up. (Laughs)

Were you in a house or building? Did you go through a roof or anything like that?

I was going up, and as I went up there were oriental designs on stone crevice walls. It was like a huge rock tower. I was in an ancient Japanese or Chinese building made from rocks and rough stone. Zeus was pulling the whole ground and tower up. Everything went up when he grabbed it.

You were in the tower?

Well, I was on my way up but not going quickly enough.

Did you finally get to where you were going?

Yes. When I got up there, I was on top of a huge rock tower, a stone tower, and everyone was up there. It was just incredible. It felt like a party.

What do you mean by saying that *everyone* was up there?

The ascended masters and good people who have done wonderful things on this Earth.

Who else did you notice up there besides Zeus?

Buddha, Saint Germain, Jesus, Mother Teresa, Gandhi, and the Dalai Lama.

The Dalai Lama was up there even though he's still alive?

Yes, he was up there too. I hung out there for a while with Buddha. I connected really well with him. I was just present there, just listening and taking it in. I didn't really speak or ask questions. I was visually excited.

Did they interact with you or were they just doing their own thing?

They were talking and laughing. They were having what seemed like a party. (Laughs)

Did you feel comfortable there?

Oh, yes. It was like I had been there a million lifetimes. It felt so natural to me.

Childhood Memories

Then I went back and saw my childhood dreams. They were significant at the time, when I was really young. I was remembering my purpose when I was a kid. I must have forgotten it over time.

The dreams were related to your purpose?

Yes, the whole of it was related to my purpose, and then growing up with certain people who are also starseeds. I was seeing my friends influence me when I was younger, pushing me in that direction, which I kind of veered off of eventually. I was seeing how the guides were plotting the starseeds' paths.

Were you seeing some kind of cosmic design?

I could see my childhood neighborhood from a bird's-eye view and I could see the starseeds being pointed out.

Did you see that the star seeds were going to connect with each other to give support to one another?

Yes, at different times. That's why they lived so close to us. That actually made me very emotional. I also saw yours and mommy's past when you were really involved with the Brotherhood of Light. It was when you met and connections were being made for both of you. I was seeing that and seeing miracles. I was really appreciative of all the people who had helped both of you along the way. I became emotional about that too.

Ancient Archers

Then I went up into a cave with two women who seemed to be from ancient mythology. All three of us were Sagittarians and kind of all-knowing, perhaps even like witches. (Laughs) We had crossbows and would shoot arrows over an ocean range. Each arrow that we shot would break an egg, and a yolk would drop.

Were any of these women related to your Atlantean life with Demetria?

Maybe. It's possible, because it was near the water. There were pterodactyls. I had a pet pterodactyl and would feed squids to it. (Laughter)

Orion's Crown of Glass

I saw you and mom when you were younger. There was a riddle that had to do with fire. You were at a ritual gathering with a fire pit and crown of glass. You kept singing a riddle or song to entice a fire being. You just kept doing that and eventually we went off into the desert. I had herbs and was singing a song. Orion was wearing a huge crown of broken glass and leading people to this gathering.

Orion was wearing a crown made of broken glass?

Yes. It looked like a priest's hat.

Was this the same Orion who had a constellation named in his honor?

Yes. He was a light worker of some sort. We went to this gathering where somebody was possessed and darting like crazy around this rock enclosure, a tight space. Orion had that crown of glass and was trying to capture the possessed being into it.

Who else was there?

Jesus, Saint Germain, and other ascended masters were all there.

Was this being just flying around the enclosure?

Yes. It was going crazy and bouncing off the walls. People all gathered and circled around it, but it had somebody working with it, too, trying to keep it going.

Somebody was helping it to remain mad?

Yes, there was a woman helping it. Orion was just trying to stay strong, to maintain a chief focus of getting it into the crown of glass. We would all sit strong for a really long time but it never ended up going into the crown of glass.

It's important to realize that no matter how strong the forces of light might be, everyone still has choices about what they're going to do.

End of the World

I also had a very sad experience where the ascended masters took me to the end of the world.

What does that mean?

They were showing me the animals that were still living on the Earth and how I had to try my hardest to get them to strive and survive, because there weren't that many animals left.

So, you're talking about sometime in the future when the planet might be in a dire condition, not the edge of the planet or universe.

Yes. It was the end of humans, and they had all these animals but they didn't know if they were going to survive. The climate changes were so drastic.

It doesn't have to be that way. It doesn't mean that's how it's going to be. Did you get the sense that was just one choice if projected out into the future? Or did you sense that is where we're heading?

I don't know. I tried to get some of the animals to thrive. Some were living in the cold, in colder regions than before, drastically cold. They were just underwater dwellers. I got them to become land and water dwellers so that they'd have these dens above the water.

What was the purpose of that? Was the water polluted?

Once winter hit, it was going to be so cold that they wouldn't survive in the water.

Why was it going to be cold if global warming caused the problem?

These were animals surviving around the only cold area. Then I came back to normal time and saw all the waste that we go through. Many people just don't care about our planet at all. We were trying to make this a biodegradable world with the surviving humans. We were trying to help each other, our neighbors, and keep the recycling going, but it wasn't working.

Biodegradable? Did you feel that this was another type of guidance that was being given to you and others?

Yes. Then I went back to Africa. My tour guide was waiting for me there. A lot of trees had been torn down from the bulldozers. He told me to go and help the elephants. I went to do it but couldn't make it. Everyone had a purpose, something that they needed to do.

Who else was on your tour?

Just me. There were others, but they were on their own tours.

Life and Death

It's time for Damiana to expand her third eye travels, to expand her comfort levels, to push forward out of her comfort zone. Move forward, continuing to do these sessions, experimenting with new concepts and ideas using imagination and creativity. Push beyond the limits of what you already know, breaking down those boundaries.

I'm in a garden. There are gardenias everywhere, white and soft pink. There are also animal bones that have been bleached in the Sun. They are all around. The colors are quite vivid. The sky is very blue. The gardenias — and even the white of the bleached bones — are very bright. It's breathtaking how vivid the colors are. If you've never seen this before, it's like living in a black and white world, then seeing color for the first time. It's incredible. The shapes and sculptures are very impressive.

I'm in some sort of an ancient burial ground for animals. They've come here to die and now it's a lovely garden. So at first it seemed like it was just a beautiful garden that was full of life, but now it has this interesting balance between life and death with all of these bones. The contrast is amazing.

What are you experiencing now?

I'm just lying here.

Are you ready to return?

I just want to lie here for a while and then I will return.

Summon the Light

Damiana Sage Miller receives messages from ascended masters, angels, archangels, benevolent extraterrestrials, and other beings of Light. For more information, visit her website:

www.SummonTheLight.com

Purchasing Information

Additional copies of *Third Eye Awakening, Adventures of a Clairvoyant Traveler* (ISBN: 978-1881217398) may be purchased from *New Atlantean Press*. Call 505-983-1856. Or send $12.95 (in U.S. funds), plus $5.00 shipping, to:

New Atlantean Press
PO Box 9638
Santa Fe, NM 87504
505-983-1856 (Telephone & Fax)
Email: think@thinkchoice.com

This book is also available at many fine bookstores:
ISBN: 978-1881217398

Bookstores/Libraries/Retail Buyers: Order from Midpoint, Baker &Taylor, Ingram, New Leaf, or New Atlantean Press.

Non-Storefront Buyers: Take a 40% discount with the purchase of 5 or more copies (multiply the total cost of purchases x .60). Please add 9% ($5.00 minimum) for shipping. *Larger discounts are available.*

Shipping: Please add 9% ($5.00 minimum) for shipping. Allow 1-3 weeks for your order to arrive, or include $2.00 extra for priority air mail shipping. **Foreign orders** should email us for rates: think@thinkchoice.com

Also Available from New Atlantean Press

Ambassadors Between Worlds, Intergalactic Gateway to a New Earth (ISBN: 978-1881217381). Conversations between enlightened extraterrestrials and their ambassador on the Earth. Topics include the nature of God, evolution of the soul, finding your purpose, living your passion, cleaning up the environment, and developing new energy resources. Code: ABW (288 p.) $15.95.

Holy Christ Revealed: The True Life of Jesus, Including Details of His Birth, Teen Years and Spiritual Mission (ISBN: 1-881217337). The words and deeds of Jesus taken from the akashic records. Includes intimate details about his birth, early childhood, teen years and spiritual mission. From the birth of Mother Mary to the trial, crucifixion and resurrection of Jesus, your heart will open and spirit quicken as the Holy Christ is revealed. Code: HCR (192 p.) $14.95.

Gadzooks! Extraterrestrial Guide to Love, Wisdom and Happiness (ISBN: 1-881217213). Extraordinary beings from other worlds offer insight, guidance, and a lyrical blueprint for your spiritual growth. Code GAD (96 p.) $9.95.

ONLINE CATALOG: *New Atlantean Press* offers a unique selection of books on spiritual inspiration and holistic health. Visit:

www.thinkchoice.com